Slice

Cutting Through to Excellence in Sales Leadership

VINIT SHAH

Slice

First published in 2019 by

Panoma Press Ltd
48 St Vincent Drive, St Albans, Herts, AL1 5SJ, UK
info@panomapress.com
www.panomapress.com

Book layout by Neil Coe.

Printed on acid-free paper from managed forests.

ISBN 978-1-784521-65-3

A CIP catalogue record for this book is available from the British Library.

This book is available online and in bookstores.

DEDICATION

My parents have never judged me and always tried to support me in the best way they could. They've provided me with a platform that has enabled me to thrive and I dedicate this book to them to say thank you for everything you have done for me and with me.

To each and every person who I've shared any interaction and experience with throughout my life, I may not have appreciated everyone or everything at that moment in time. However, I'm learning to live in the moment more and this book is also to acknowledge and say thank you, because without those moments we've shared I may not have been inspired to take action and share my thoughts.

Finally, if I have knowingly or unknowingly hurt anyone then I take this opportunity to say sorry and ask for forgiveness. As we say in Jainism – Michhami Dukkadam to you all.

CONTENTS

INTRODUCTION

Over the last 20 years that I have been involved in sales, the art of selling has evolved significantly, and whilst the sales industry had an indifferent reputation many years ago, it's now front and centre to the success of every business. The plethora of choice and freely available information means buyers in all industries are inundated with requests to sample or trial products, and as such the function of sales is shifting from consultative into the realm of advisory. This transition is taking place alongside innovations in technology that will automate processes and the emergence of smart artificial intelligence that will enhance the role that sales advisors will provide to their customers and prospects. These changes will over time lead to transactional aspects of a salesperson's role to become redundant, whilst the need for innovation, strong leadership, better management of processes and talent will be required more than ever to transform the industry and help businesses achieve the growth and desired outcomes sought.

I wrote this book as a reference to help aspiring salespeople that want to lead, manage or take control of their own development. Those that want to cut through the noise and differentiate themselves from focusing solely on traditional sales management theories. The topics covered may also be of interest to individuals working alongside sales teams and looking for opportunities to better understand how to positively influence their colleagues' performance and growth.

Whilst it's based on my experiences and observations, the topics have been discussed with sales professionals from a range of companies. The messages resonate because the challenges we face today are similar irrespective of the nuances of the industries we operate in. The individuals we want to manage, lead and inspire are all looking for direction. The carrot and stick approach needs to be progressed to make considerations for new challenges that have emerged. True success comes from understanding not only yourself but the individuals that work with you and around you. Their needs are constantly evolving and hence they need to be engaged in a more thoughtful way which motivates them to realise their growth potential.

It is for this reason that I'm cutting straight through and tackling more emotive, mindful and behavioural subjects that have historically never been given the credence that they deserve within sales organisations let alone businesses more generally. Key themes and areas of focus include:

- The importance of personal vision and commitment
- Appreciating your values, their origin and how they impact on you each day
- Considering different perspectives and reducing the number of assumptions you make
- The importance of self-actualisation and its continued influence on situations
- Identifying the habits that are impacting on your growth and implementing change
- Why everything you do impacts on your character

More than 10 years of my career have been in management and leadership roles. I've developed numerous individuals, teams and have a proven track record in delivering positive results and outcomes. I've fine-tuned my skills and appreciate what it takes to succeed. I practise a style of management and leadership that empowers individuals to experiment, pushing any boundaries that may exist whilst harnessing the power that is present within them to progressively endeavour to do the best they possibly can. Rather than just focusing on outputs and results, every salesperson, manager and leader must be obsessed with understanding the various inputs, perspectives and knowledge they are ingesting and how these are being processed within them in accordance with their values and emotional biases. The better we're all able to understand ourselves and accept who we are, the less likely we are to negotiate with ourselves whilst developing at a faster pace and realising our growth potential.

For reasons of anonymity and confidentiality I have changed names of individuals and adjusted details of certain situations; however, the material facts and connotations are an accurate account of what happened from my point of view. My hope is that my observations and insights provoke your own reflective practice where you contemplate your own situation and identify how you and those around you can grow more effectively whilst building a character that makes you stand out from the crowd.

I encourage everyone to embrace their difference, diversity and awaken the sleeping giant that resides within you to unleash your power to maximise your growth potential.

Chapter 1

ACKNOWLEDGING WHERE YOU ARE

In one form or another I have been involved in selling or sales-related roles since the age of 10. Life has been interesting and provided me with many lessons, which due to my failure to comprehend at times has meant the need to have them played back repeatedly until I've managed to fully understand and learn from them. That is par for the course for many of us no doubt and it takes hindsight to realise what you need to change in order to move forward. I've learned to accept and value myself as well as embracing each experience as a blessing that I need to go through to help my continuous development and progression.

Whilst this is a business-related book focused on the wonderful world of sales, a little bit of information about my journey will help provide context and understanding of my thought process and the origin of some of the topics covered. Over time I've learned to accept that everything happens for the best, and whilst when you're in the eye of the storm it never looks that way, there always seems to be something better beyond the horizon. The storms are sometimes a necessary evil to help you learn as well as navigating you in the direction needed to support your future growth and development.

My first experience of sales was working in the family business which sold a range of fast-moving consumer goods through a retail store. From a young age I learned how to converse with customers, promote benefits of products, and help them with making considered choices. At the age of 11 I shared a morning newspaper round with my sisters where the three of us alternated the round between us each week. I built a good relationship with the manager at the newsagents and over time took on the responsibility of opening the store as well as working there on weekends and school holidays. As my need for material things increased in my teenage years, I added working at a bowling alley on weekends to my list of jobs. From a young age I had my financial independence and spent most of what I earned, the idea of saving was never considered to be important. I eventually quit the different jobs a week before I started university. Looking back, it's not hard to see why I didn't achieve the grades I was capable of at school, but I have no regrets!

At university, I found a job within a call centre selling prepaid newspaper subscriptions. I didn't make the same mistake though and this time concentrated on my studies. However, that did leave me with a significant debt when I finished university, which is where the real story of my career in sales began and was sandwiched between a tragic event that shaped a lot of my thinking, behaviour and outlook.

My first full-time job was at Technicolor, who at the time manufactured VHS cassettes and later went on to be, and still are, the biggest manufacturer of DVDs and DVD games in the world for various Hollywood studios and games publishers. I enjoyed eight fantastic years there and was involved in several commercial roles ranging from client administration to sales management.

It was during my time at Technicolor that I fell in love and was supposed to get married in the summer of 2008, but tragically my fiancée's father was killed in a robbery. She was devastated, and a lot was changing in her life and within her. I decided to quit my job and fly to the other side of the world to be with her; however, after seven or eight months, things had changed, and she needed her own space and time to grieve and connect with herself. Shortly after I returned home, she was diagnosed with breast cancer, and has been through a challenging few years having to go through chemotherapy and a double mastectomy. Whilst we're not in contact any more, I have nothing but the deepest admiration for her, and if anyone deserves a bright light to be shined on them then it's her.

The impact of her father's death and subsequent events tore through me. My life had disintegrated in front of me. I was close to her father although I had only known him for a short time. Her mum had passed away when she was 10, with breast cancer, and so her dad played a prominent role in her upbringing and that of her younger sister. I didn't realise the impact losing her would have on me. I did some crazy things during and after this time and was staring at the abyss of a black hole for a long time. I didn't want to see anyone or be around anyone. My finances were all over the place and as a consequence of being unemployed I had to sign on the dole.

The process of picking myself up was a long journey and a lot of it now is a blur. It was after 50 or so job interviews and close to a year going by before I managed to get a job. In hindsight, I had been very selfish because I was thinking about myself and not the grief, suffering and pain that she was going through. I've come a long way since then, but that experience taught me more about myself and about what is and isn't important in life. The context of why this story is important will make sense as you digest the content and themes of the chapters that follow.

So, as I mentioned, my career was sandwiched between those events. I landed a job at Mintel, the consumer market research specialist. I was just happy to get the job because at the time I only had money left in my account for bills etc for around one month. I hadn't told anyone in my family or my friends about my financial situation and look back now in amazement at what I had done.

Tragic things happen every day, and unless it impacts us directly, we tend to let the thought pass us by and carry on. We're happy to acknowledge it, but to some degree happy that it isn't us that is going through that. However, knowing this still doesn't stop us from judging those around us, and who's to say that they aren't going through their own life-changing event.

This book is somewhat of a stocktake to detail what has helped me to become successful and I hope anyone that reads it is inspired to realise their own potential. When you open your eyes and see things from a different perspective, the opportunities you create for yourself and those around you are truly amazing.

I've had to work hard to achieve what I have and believe that everything I have been through has prepared me for the amazing things that will come next.

Be ruthless if you want to grow

When you start focusing on trying to understand yourself more and conduct an introspective assessment where you are ruthless about your positive and negative attributes, you realise exactly where you are versus the image you may have been outwardly displaying. Nobody wants to think of themselves as not being capable or lacking certain skills; however, failure to acknowledge your fallibility is a big reason why many individuals struggle to realise and fulfil their potential.

A good way to start this evaluation is by conducting a personal SWOT analysis. This type of analysis is typically used in business as a strategic planning technique to identify strengths, weaknesses, opportunities and threats related to business competition or project planning. Applying the concept on an individual level helps identify the internal and external factors that one sees as favourable or unfavourable in oneself.

I was once asked to prepare a personal SWOT for an interview to help the prospective business understand where I would need development. Through completing the process I realised it was a powerful tool for self-assessment as well as developing personal and strategic growth goals. The assessment allowed me to harness my strengths and leverage those whilst working on the elements that were less developed and needed evolving.

You will rarely find individuals within a sales organisation that don't want to grow, but many don't fulfil their potential because they fail to take control of their development and acknowledge why they are where they are. They do not proactively pursue the acquisition of skills needed to achieve the promotion into diverse commercial roles, and most importantly they are happy to abdicate the responsibility for their development to their line manager hoping they will connect the dots for them. Whilst many good managers will help individuals, without the right engagement and commitment on both sides it's unlikely that the end result will achieve the intended objectives. There is no fast track route to success. The process for each individual is different, requires hard work, dedication and a personal commitment which starts with understanding yourself better than anyone else.

The capacity for growth is available to everyone, however in order to activate it everyone must look within themselves. When a person doesn't take time to assess themselves, they tend to act on impulse or default to following the general trends that they see around them, which leads to jumping from one thing to the next without any strategic rationale. Better decisions are made following reflection and understanding the positive or negative impact whilst considering the desired outcomes sought in every situation.

Understanding yourself better

The impact of an experience is felt differently by each person, and although we've all probably been through something similar that we can relate to, we can never suggest that the feelings we're going through are in any way the same. There might be some similarities, however they will likely elicit very different emotional responses and reactions in everyone. Whilst it's never easy when you're going through these challenging moments, every cloud has a silver lining, and for me this event was the start of taking control and building myself back from the bottom up and developing a version of myself that I was happy with and wanted to be.

I acknowledge that I don't know everything, and I will never know everything, however my reflex now is to continuously focus on improving myself. I don't just mean from a business perspective, but from a personal perspective too. I am focused on doing the absolute best I can until I know better, and then I owe it to myself to use that knowledge and apply it to improving myself.

My daily practice of reflection has helped me understand trends and my own bias towards situations and individuals as well as improving my engagement with those around me. Prior to having this daily practice, I used to get agitated when things didn't go to plan and would make my annoyance known to those around me. Since adopting this practice I am a lot calmer and able to see things from a range of perspectives as opposed to just my own limited view.

I'm an advocate of personal development, and through completing numerous self-awareness tests I've managed to learn more about myself. If you're committed to your development, then I would encourage you to take tests like the ones listed below:

- The personality style test (amiable, analytical, driver and expressive – I am a driver)

- 360-degree test where friends and colleagues score you (provides some interesting context on how those around you see you)

- Interpersonal skills test (listening, verbal communication, emotional intelligence, impact of working in teams)

- Grit Score by Angela Duckworth – a measure of how likely you are to see things through

You can't change everything overnight. It's a gradual process that requires your commitment and investment into you. Acknowledging who you are and allowing yourself that room to develop helps improve you as a person, manager and leader. Knowledge is great; however, understanding when and how to use it to generate the desired impact and results for yourself and those around you is the equivalent of being an alchemist in leadership terms.

What causes your progress to be hindered

Early in my career, personal development stalled because I lacked self-belief. I was consciously anxious and never felt confident, especially in a team setting where I was exposed. I was always worried about saying the wrong thing and fearful about getting asked questions that I may not know the answer to. This fear of how it would look in front of the team had held me back.

If I had known then what I know now, I really wouldn't have worried, but then hindsight is a wonderful thing! It's ironic that those who seem to know it all, and constantly criticise or challenge those around them, are actually the ones that are in denial and cannot cope with change, and lack the ability to think differently.

Through managing and leading teams, I've been exposed to various scenarios which have impacted on an individual's development. Whilst it's not my place to judge the situation or reasons why, what

I do find interesting is how something that is easy for one person to deal with can be a significant challenge for someone else. You can never second guess a situation or scenario and assume that just because it worked for one individual it will work for another. Furthermore, when we go through any trauma (at work or at home), we all react to it in different ways. Sometimes that trauma is a catalyst for subconscious thoughts and fears to come to a head causing self-doubt and uncertainty, which ultimately can lead to progress and growth being hampered.

One of my biggest bugbears is when someone talks a great game but then fails to follow it up and deliver. They've done the hard work and don't realise the negative impact their behaviour can have. One time a supplier (Geraint) was coming in to meet my boss and me for the annual business review. The meeting went very well, and Geraint had some great new ideas which we supported and felt would add value. We left that meeting in a positive frame of mind hoping what Geraint had proposed would support the development of our partnership further. However, after the meeting we waited for a few days and nothing happened: no follow-up and no action plan. My boss and I were left confused and disappointed to say the least. If you say you're going to do something, then make sure you do it as your reputation is at stake!

Getting to the next level of development

The road to developing yourself and those around you is a continuous process and not one that you can allocate any definite time to. What takes one person a few weeks to understand, practise and master can take someone else a few months or even longer. You cannot compare yourself to anyone else, and in my opinion the key elements that an individual needs to fulfil their potential are: desire, motivation, belief and above all the right attitude.

I consider these elements to be important because they are crucial in supporting growth and helping individuals through the different phases of their personal development process. We all go through this process but maybe don't give it as much thought and credence as it deserves. There is no set process or series of steps or phases, however categorising them as such helps to ensure you're asking the right questions of yourself. I typically break down the phases as: doubt, excitement, questioning, experimenting and acceptance.

A successful local businessman, Sonny, was telling me about his personal experience of his mother suffering with a chronic illness for 30 years before passing away in his arms. Since his mother's death Sonny felt something wasn't right and he was compelled to sign up to a 12-week personal development programme where he started seeing a specialist development coach to help him understand himself better. Sonny recalled on one of the first sessions the coach asking, "How are you today?" Sonny glumly said, "Look at the weather, it's raining and miserable, a bit like how I feel." The coach replied, "But just imagine how amazing your garden will look tomorrow." Sonny was taken back by the response, he'd never considered or seen it in that way, and so the process of self-actualisation began. Seeing the best in every situation not only makes you feel more positive and optimistic but breeds opportunities. Your inner reflex is focused on growth and progression rather than negative thoughts of doom and gloom.

Personal strategy and sacrifice

If you accept that you are the master of your destiny, then it's important for you to determine your own vision, goals and objectives, just like any business or department would. In order to realise those ambitions some sacrifices will be needed.

I believe in the power of visualisation and channelling my energy to support growth. I like to dream and let my mind wander sometimes – it's healthy and takes away the monotony of what we do every day. The information that I have filed in my subconscious needs to be processed and visualisation can help with this. If you close your eyes and visualise what success looks like, you will see yourself in the future: not tomorrow, not next week and not even next year but several years from now, an aspirational vision of yourself. A subconscious vision of yourself. You can choose to believe whatever you see or not, as the case may be. You may have doubts and think, it makes no sense, I can't see myself doing that. However, I find that when I do this my visualisations sometimes show me the sacrifices that may need to be made in order to realise my aspirations. I accept that it might seem a little 'out there', however we all need to let go sometimes and dream a little more as we did when we were children and take a leap of faith to realise our potential.

When I have historically identified what I want to achieve and go after it, anything that I have had to give up or decided not to carry on with has never felt like a sacrifice. It's more like ending something that no longer serves me and moving in a new direction towards something that is going to help me accomplish my ambitions.

The importance of vision, goals and objectives

Whilst vision is an aspirational process, the goals (desired outcomes) and objectives can help you bring that to life. More importantly, these three elements help you to paint a picture for those around you which becomes like a journey that you're taking together. Whilst it would be fantastic for those around you to accept your vision as theirs, they may not be thinking in the same deep and meaningful way that you are, and as such need to find a connection that helps them on that journey.

When you don't have a vision that you're working towards, you could be fulfilling activities that are based on someone else's ideas. You may not be entirely convinced with those ideas or the execution, but because you haven't identified your own goals you are happy to accept those ideas as your own for the time being. If, however, you have a strong mental image of where you see yourself, your team or the business in the future, you're likely to have clear direction and everything you do or say will (consciously and subconsciously) be working towards attainment of that vision. You're more likely to start setting goals and subsequently objectives, or sub goals, that performance can be measured against.

When setting objectives it's equally important to identify expected results and measure of success. You could argue and say but you don't always know what results you're going to achieve, and yes that's true; however, you will intuitively have an idea of the direction, and setting even a small target is better than not setting one. What's the worst that can happen if you set a target and then don't achieve it? You've learned something, adjusted your position and you continue to move forward.

Making sacrifices

This is a question that I have mulled over time and time again and, in short, yes, sacrifice is necessary. However, it's not the process of making a sacrifice that's important, it's the conscious acknowledgement that you've realised that you need to make a change in order to achieve your vision, goals and objectives. Simple sacrifices like not going for that night out are also important, but it's about choosing you and yourself above the alternatives that are on offer.

An old client, Harry, is a property developer who shared an interesting story with me about how he imagined things would pan out versus how things turned out. From his early 20s Harry was committed to setting up his own business, and whilst many of his friends were out most evenings and weekends socialising, Harry spent his time working and laying the foundations to get his business off the ground. Harry had made a conscious choice to invest his time in what he deemed to be more important and a priority to him rather than socialising. Harry's vision from an early age was to retire by the age of 50, and in order to achieve this he was willing to make the necessary sacrifices that he felt would not support this vision.

When telling me the story, Harry was in his 50s, and did he achieve his targets? To some degree. Whilst Harry was way ahead of his close friends when it came to business, in sacrificing social time and prioritising his business he lost touch with numerous friends, and over time personal relationships changed. He regrets this and acknowledges that whilst the business was a priority, he should have made time for his friends.

Harry got married when he was in his 30s and had a couple of kids along the way. It was only when he met his wife that he realised there is a balance that needs to be struck when you're striving towards your goals. Harry had to make a number of compromises, which on reflection he's so happy that he made because it was in those moments that he realised how important having loved ones around you is. He regrets losing contact with his friends, and even though he's reconnected with some of them, the relationships haven't been the same. Harry runs an established property management company now, and would love to turn back time and give his young self some different advice from the course of action he took. So, whilst sacrifice is necessary, a careful balance needs to be struck to ensure that it does not cause future regret.

Clarity and execution

Simply put, vision without clarity of thought, execution and desire will go nowhere and instead remain as just another idea. Having this level of clarity is important. I'm not saying that everything must go to plan and be mapped out; however, you need to have a firm idea of what you want and how you want to go about getting there. If you chase the vision without a plan you will move from idea to idea without ever achieving any of them.

Having that strong purpose and clarity in not only what you want to do but an idea of how you are going to go about it is crucial if you want your vision, goals and objectives to manifest successfully in the future.

A close friend, Tim, from high school who now works in the creative media industry has always been full of incredible ideas and is great at starting projects but never seems to be able to see them through. He convinced 10 of us high school buddies, and got us excited about setting up a charity to help kids at our old school that had difficulties at home and couldn't afford the same equipment or trips as other kids. Great idea and we all backed it. Set up the joint charity bank account and were ready to go. As always though with Tim, it lacked the necessary planning to execute his vision and soon enough we gave whatever money was in the account to the school and returned the rest to the donors.

You may be thinking why others in the group didn't help, and you're right; with hindsight we should all have got more involved, but at the time it was Tim's vision and that's what we bought into. To some degree we were all waiting for him to determine the plan, and when that didn't materialise, the noble idea lost momentum. Many years later, Tim has started his own business, and he's now successful because he has acknowledged where his limitations were and has proactively got help to improve in those areas.

Have a powerful and inspiring 'why'

Not wanting to steal any thunder from Simon Sinek, but having a powerful and inspiring 'why' is so important. As he states, "… because in business it doesn't matter what you do, it matters why you do it."

My why is that I want to share my knowledge and experience to help individuals and businesses grow and compete where they didn't think they could. In the same way that I was afforded a second chance, I want to give back and help individuals realise their potential and how amazing they already are and can be if they believe in themselves.

Wake up and smell the coffee

Since a young age I aspired to have my own business. And over the years I evaluated various business opportunities but was never interested in the products or services that I came across. When I hit the ripe old age of 40, I started to think that the opportunity to own and run my own business had gone. However, during a period of personal assessment and reflection I came to the realisation that I am the product. My knowledge and experience within sales is valuable and could be used to help individuals and businesses unlock their growth potential.

I set up Vintus Consulting, which has been an exciting journey and given me a new sense of purpose. I'm learning lots and being challenged in different ways each day. However, the buzz I get from going into businesses and helping them transform their sales strategy, processes and subsequently implementing change programmes makes getting up each day worthwhile.

Appreciating your passion

Passion is an extremely important emotion, and one that everyone needs to both have and understand the impact of. It is the emotional catalyst that helps you realise your vision, growth and inspiration, and sets you apart from every other idea or individual out there. It's your energy and devotion to what you want to bring to life that makes the vision so powerful.

In the same way you must be interested in whatever you're doing to generate that commitment to success, passion is the driving force. My passion is my focus on continuous improvement and my desire to grow my business and those that I work with. I am passionate about doing things in the right way, that promotes good business practice whilst balancing the needs of the individuals that I work with and for.

Doing it for the right reasons

Whatever your focus personally or professionally, you must ensure that you're doing it for the right reasons and not just for the sake of it. Many friends and colleagues have suggested that they are working simply to earn money, pay the bills, enjoy holidays etc. Whilst I can see why they look at things in this way, I believe it's restricting their ability to maximise their potential. I appreciate that it's easy for me to say and each circumstance is different, but if you approach it with a different mindset then it can completely change your outlook on life and the results you will achieve.

When I first started working full time, I was quite negative about the job I had and questioned what good it would do for me. This attitude and mindset stunted my progress. It wasn't until I changed my outlook that I realised how important those experiences were for my development. They laid the foundation for my growth and helped me overcome some of the basic challenges that I had. Now I have trained myself to accept and look at each job differently, and when I refer to 'job' I am also talking about the role you are sometimes asked to do as part of a team.

If it's something I have done previously then it's an opportunity to use my experience and test my knowledge; if it's something new then the likelihood is that I'll need to learn a new skill or connect with individuals that may have better knowledge than I do. Either way I see it as an opportunity to develop. If you start with the right attitude and an open mind, you will be successful, and it will help you with realising your ultimate objective. On the flip side, if you don't put the right energy and effort into the role then the result will be average and you're not likely to inspire those around you.

You've heard it before, everyone has a choice

No matter what, we all have a choice. In every situation, in every conversation and in every action that we perform we have a choice. There are consequences of those choices and we need to be comfortable with the possible outcomes or the unknowns that may follow, but it's down to us. It's easy to blame others for putting you in an uncomfortable position where you are required to make a choice that you're not entirely comfortable with; however, that event is probably the cause of several previous actions or activities that have taken place. When we are faced with those situations we focus so much in that moment and lose sight of why we are in that situation in the first place. I accept that individual circumstance plays a role, but no matter how tough the situation or decision you are required to take, you still always have a choice.

There is an inherent worry whenever we make a choice. Will it turn out OK? What will happen if things don't work out? This is our mind playing games with us. We must learn to control our mind, condition and programme it. In my opinion, worrying is the biggest waste of time because what good does it do? It takes all the joy away and you're left feeling drained. If you believe in who you are and what you're doing, you will make the balanced decision that is right for you, your team and the situation that you find yourself in. When something is in your control, do something about it; if not, try and influence it if you can. Where things are not in your control, hope for the best but plan for the possibilities and prepare yourself rather than worrying.

When I decided to leave my job and set up my own business, I was faced with a huge dilemma. I had an incredible job, a well-performing team, great colleagues and opportunities to get involved in various strategic projects. However, at that moment in time, I had to decide whether I stayed in a comfortable environment, which I loved and had provided me with lots of success, or whether to take the bold decision to quit and set up my own business. Whilst I had the drive, energy and experience there were a lot of unknowns that I had to deal with. The key thing was that I programmed myself to accept that there would be challenges along the way and was open to learning. I was aware that there would be uncomfortable moments where I wouldn't know what to do, and I accepted that I may need to make sacrifices and further changes to my lifestyle to realise my dream. I pre-programmed my mind to be ready to handle the unknown. You can never be 100% ready, but I had created a mechanism for myself to deal with whatever came next. It was a tough choice leaving security, structure and familiarity behind for a new venture where success wasn't guaranteed.

Between a rock and a hard place

When making any decisions it can be difficult and increase anxiety, blood pressure, and in some instances get people downbeat because they don't like having that burden placed on them. However, when you do make tough decisions consistently you start accepting a higher standard. Tough decisions will rarely yield quick results. When you take a decision that sometimes goes against what others might want, you do so because you believe it's the right thing to do. Others may not have access to all the information and context that you do. Whatever happens, making the tough call will grow you.

When I first went into sales management, I was responsible for a small team of three individuals. I took a few weeks to get to know them, how they worked, understand their motivations, concerns etc. I had a few choices: the easy one would have been to change nothing and carry on as the team was doing OK. However, in my mind that was the wrong thing to do. Based on my conversations with them, the objectives my boss had set me, the potential challenges that I could see coming down the line and my personal objectives, I decided to restructure the team. In the short term there was turmoil and change for the team. I learned a lot about myself, how to communicate more effectively and was thrown several curve balls that I hadn't considered. I was lucky; my boss backed my decision and helped me see the change through. Short-term pain resulted in a better structure, and in the medium term, results improved as did the team's morale and output.

Consequences of what you decide

There are times when you may have to take a short-term view, however you need to ensure that you do this with your eyes wide open and scenarios mapped out. You will see quick results, which in a target-driven industry are sometimes what you need. However, they can have a knock-on effect as teams and businesses can become used to working for short-term results whilst not thinking about the bigger picture.

When working in a call centre I was making outbound calls selling a discounted subscription package for a national newspaper group. The team was targeted daily, and hence the closer it got to the end of the day, the level of discounting increased. Whilst the business achieved the results it needed to, and the strategy worked for the short term, the level of discounting was unsustainable. Additionally, in that environment the mindset of the salespeople changed over time. We were paid commission on the volume of sales made, so if we could offer a larger discount and get a quicker sale then why would we want to spend longer than necessary trying to close the sale?

When making choices that provide short-term success or results you must be careful to acknowledge what the impact will be on an ongoing basis and how you will manage this. Once you make a choice that yields short-term success and results it can become very easy to continue to implement this strategy as results are tangible. However, there is a long-term impact that can have lasting consequences and be damaging for the salesperson, the team and the business's strategy.

It's OK to ask for help

Is it wrong to ask for help? Can it be seen as a weakness? For a long time I used to struggle with asking anyone for help. In my mind I felt that if I had been given a job to do it was because I had the necessary skills to do it and therefore I shouldn't need to ask anyone for help. As I took on more responsibility, I realised that not asking for help was a weakness of mine, and over time as I've managed other managers, I've observed it to be a significant weakness of many sales managers. When you're promoted to any role there is sometimes a sense that from day one you should be doing whatever the role requires you to do, and the reality is that is just not the case. You've been promoted because you have the right attributes and attitude to be successful; however, you don't start that job as the finished article.

When you understand your limitations and subsequently are open to receiving help to progress, you will see it as a positive step. Getting help is an empowering feeling. It keeps you in check and creates a bond with your team, your manager and others around you. It will help you understand something that you may not have considered whilst creating rapport and trust.

Recalling when my line manager broached this subject, he simply said it's OK to ask for help and not thinking that you have to do it all yourself. It was an important lesson and sound advice. I had put so much pressure on myself that I was creating a void within the team environment and needed to readdress this balance. By asking for help from individuals within the team they became more involved and took greater ownership whilst feeling empowered. It sounds so trivial, yet sometimes it's those small things that generate the greatest impact.

Helping yourself

Asking for help is you helping yourself. If you don't ask for help and instead make decisions based on your ego, fear or not knowing how to ask, you're failing yourself and putting your potential for growth at risk as well as jeopardising the relationship with your team and their potential.

A piece of advice that I used to give the managers that worked for me was if you can't help yourself how can you help anyone else? If you don't realise when you need help, how will you ever be able to see when your team needs help and support? Different people will have different ideas and perspectives and you may not agree with all that you hear; however, those different viewpoints will help shape your thinking and develop a better solution with clarity, especially when there is confusion or a lack of understanding.

Trying to do it all yourself

When you try to do everything yourself, the likelihood is that you will spread yourself too thinly and not do any of it to the best of your ability. In short bursts of time you can dedicate yourself to taking on additional responsibilities and tasks to firefight issues at hand, but this strategy will be extremely challenging to maintain for a long period of time. You need to have clear timeframes and objectives for what you're going to do and by when.

From experience, if you try to do it all yourself, at some point your health will suffer, you will put additional strain on your personal relationships, and on occasion, a siege mentality can also set in where you become so involved that you fail to see the ongoing impact of what you're doing or what's happening around you.

Whilst you can spin and manage multiple plates you need to prioritise what's important and remember to delegate and get help. As a manager and leader, you're wearing multiple hats already.

One of those is to develop your successor, as if you have aspirations to grow and take on additional responsibilities, then others around you need to gather the relevant experience too.

Chapter 1 Reflection Time

1. Complete personal SWOT to understand the internal and external factors you see as favourable or unfavourable within yourself.

2. Consider taking self-awareness tests as listed in the chapter to help improve your understanding of yourself.

3. Identify what your personal vision is along with the associated goals and objectives. What sacrifices do you need to make to support attainment of that vision?

4. Identify your why. What gets you out of bed each morning? Write it down and reflect on how important it is to you.

Chapter 2

ACCEPTING CHANGE IS A NECESSITY FOR GROWTH

Without change there can be no progress, development or growth. To realise your potential, you must accept that some things will have to change. This change can have a psychologically negative impact on most individuals because as human beings we tend to be creatures of habit, and once a behaviour is formed, we're reluctant to alter it.

I believe that this is a type of conditioning and programming that we put ourselves through over time, and unless there is a motivation for a specific reason of our own reckoning, we will remain reluctant to modify the behaviour significantly. In order to realise your potential, you must change your outlook and develop a new way of thinking.

Everything I do either serves to grow me and pushes me forward, or where I don't alter my behaviour it's holding my development back. If you're able to recognise what is holding you back, you start the process of accepting what needs to change. If you are motivated enough to grow and achieve your potential, you will find a way to overcome those challenges and make the necessary changes, regardless of how difficult they look.

Embracing change

Change for the sales organisation and salesperson should be a constant and, in my opinion, be seen as a positive. Whilst many sales leaders accept this, the challenge they face is developing a culture where teams embrace change and are proactively developing strategies to maximise future opportunities, at the same time as evolving the sales process. The pace of acceptance and execution can determine the impact on results, and if managed well will ensure growth for the business, its salesforce and the customer.

It can be overwhelming when you're constantly bombarded with change, however using instances of change in a positive way can create opportunity for you, your team and the business. When change happens, it's an opening to review what the team has been doing and assess whether it's still fit for purpose. Without this review and assessment, the team may continue to follow a process or maintain a behaviour that no longer serves the purpose it was intended for and subsequently it starts having a negative impact on performance. You need to be constantly curious and ask yourself and your team why they're doing what they are and whether it is still relevant or could be done differently.

Change may create some short-term perceived negative impact, but with the right planning, process variation and communication, the opportunity to evaluate your proposition and manage the sale in accordance with what customers need and how the market is evolving will be maintained.

When there has been uncertainty in the financial markets, the consequential changes needed and impact have been seen on businesses as being a negative. However, if every business saw it this way no one would gain anything from it. The individuals and businesses that succeed in those testing times are the ones that see it as an opportunity to innovate and focus on evaluating the impact and how the needs of their customers have evolved. By doing this they can adjust their proposition, story and pricing in line with what the customer is now looking for. If you view it negatively and decide not to change and just focus on price, you're not addressing the issue and are masking the problem, which over time will have a deeper impact on the business and the sales team.

Perpetual development

When external factors that are outside of your control are at play you cannot always control the pace of change, however you can control your thought reflex towards the issue and how you manage the situation. I don't believe you need to have an answer for every change that is needed, and instead what is more important is to develop a process that enables you to assess the potential impact of the change whilst modelling outcomes against the desired results.

I developed the simple, yet effective process outlined below to evaluate the potential impact of changes:

1. Collect all necessary information – talk to your team, your network, your customers and understand the impact of the change from the different viewpoints available.

2. Assess the risk factors (people, process, strategy, service, etc) associated with the change and model out the various scenarios, timings and potential results.

3. Understand the assumptions that you have made – are you able to get further clarification to improve the model you have created?

4. Evaluate each option in line with the vision, goals and objectives of the business and team.

I found that this approach supported me in getting comfortable with the information related to what was on the horizon and using that to understand the positive impact the change could bring. This approach also formed the basis for developing the tactical response needed to discuss the change with my team and others within the business. In my experience you don't need to have all the answers, however collecting the information and modelling scenarios allows you to react quickly no matter how things evolve.

I believe there are three priorities that need to be considered for any change to have a positive impact:

1. How do you personally feel about it? The likelihood is that there will be some changes that you're enthused about and others that you can't see the value of. Regardless of whether you like it or not, you must find a way of creating a positive story. Even when you're not entirely convinced by the change you must shift your thinking and consider the wider business and your team. If it's ultimately in the best interests of the business and the team longer term then you must embrace it and put your emotional bias to one side.

2. When you're talking to people about the change be open to understanding their points of view. Not everyone will embrace the change like you and listening to their specific challenges and objectives will help you formulate a more robust strategy and operational plan. Use the diversity of your network to appreciate the different perspectives and in generating ideas.

3. Change is managed best when there is consistent communication and where the team are involved throughout the process. Engagement through the use of brainstorming sessions to discuss the issue as a group and role-playing scenarios to identify potential solutions is a great way to get the team involved in the decision-making

> process. The earlier you involve them in the process, the better their understanding will be and the more time they have to get used to the potential change.

On many occasions I used to feel uncomfortable during the change cycle and there were moments of doubt, which is normal as I didn't have all the answers or a crystal ball to know how things would pan out. With experience I was able to mitigate risks earlier and understand the impact better; however, there is always an element of uncertainty and risk with any change being implemented. That uncomfortable feeling supports your development, growth and focuses your mind.

Dealing with the barriers

Once you change your mindset on how to react and respond to change, the process of dealing with the barriers becomes easier. The biggest barrier will typically be individuals within your team, who don't have the understanding or appreciation of why the change is positive. Talking to these individuals on a one to one basis and addressing their concerns is the best way to help them through the change. More often than not, it will take several conversations and for them to become comfortable with the idea, whilst going through their own internal process of accepting the change and addressing its direct impact on them. Through understanding their concerns, providing context and highlighting the benefits which they may not have considered, you're helping them to be more comfortable with the process. There is no guarantee that they will accept the change, however as a change agent sometimes there is a limit to how much you can do.

On the numerous instances where I implemented changes in structure, sales process or sales strategy it was successful because I managed to address the negative thoughts that were flowing through an individual's mind. I found that the team will start thinking about what it means for them personally and what they will need to change. At that initial stage they tend to worry less about the wider business or why the change is needed for the greater good of the team. As a result, if you address the concerns that they personally have about the change and its impact on them, you have a better chance of success. If on the other hand you're unable to identify with the concern or don't address the issues then, whilst the salesperson may accept the change, they will not be convinced by it, the doubt will remain, and they will lack the necessary understanding.

I was an advocate of encouraging my team to question anything that they were unhappy with, didn't agree with or understand. This openness was critical and extremely important in ensuring that they had clarity with regard to why certain changes were needed and the positive impact it would have on them.

On many occasions I remember my boss and I discussing changes that needed to be made in my team because of broader business challenges and the impact competitors were making. I knew some of the proposed changes would receive a positive reaction whilst others I was unsure and unconvinced about. Irrespective of my personal bias, I would always try to understand what the objective was and the desired outcomes that were sought. I felt that if I knew the answers to these two questions then I would be able to design and develop better models and solutions to facilitate the change for my team.

My boss and I disagreed on changes from time to time. This was healthy and provided an opportunity for us to understand each other's perspective and develop a more robust solution. If there was an impasse, we would park it, involve other colleagues or review what we were trying to do. We both understood that without mutual agreement and understanding there was no point pushing forward with the change as we weren't convinced.

Another strategy I often adopted was to approach the person who was the complete opposite to me and my way of thinking on the team. In doing so I achieved two things: I was able to inform the individual of the change in advance to ensure that they started to think about it; and I managed to understand their initial concerns and ensure that I developed my communication addressing those concerns, and highlighting the benefits with those specific barriers and others in mind.

Standing still

Markets, environment, people, systems, technology etc are all evolving around us and if you're not taking steps to grow in line with what's changing then you're likely to be left behind and may even find yourself standing still. Whilst fundamentals of sales will not change, if you don't move with the times then there is a risk that you will struggle to embrace future changes.

There was a lady, Jackie, who had worked in one team for 20 years. She managed a part of the business which was maintained outside of process and was reliant on her to manually control with limited use of technology or IT systems. Jackie was happy to have the autonomy and work in this way; she enjoyed her job and knew what was expected of her.

As Jackie's side of the business grew, it became impractical to manage outside of process and the department head decided that automation was needed to align with the rest of the business. For 20 years Jackie had managed the process manually without any systems or the need for external help; now suddenly, she was surrounded by members of other teams who were less than half her age and who were trying to train her on how the new process and systems should be implemented and managed. Jackie felt disgruntled. She had not been consulted on the change but was expected to implement the new systems, automate the process and work in a way that was unnatural to her. Whilst she maintained her professionalism, inside she lacked the understanding for why the decision had been made, and for the first time in 20 years was considering leaving the company because she no longer felt appreciated.

Both Jackie and the company hadn't evolved, managed communication or the change well enough. For Jackie, she hadn't considered the importance of learning the new technologies or systems that were being adopted by other teams, and the business had failed to provide Jackie with adequate training and development to make the necessary transition smooth. This situation could and should have been avoided. The business should have addressed Jackie's needs and helped her manage the change or developed her skills and understanding well in advance of the change. At the same time Jackie should have embraced some of the changes earlier and requested interaction with systems, training etc to ensure her knowledge was up to date.

There is sometimes a mentality within businesses and some teams that 'if it ain't broke, don't fix it'. The reality is that if you don't continuously focus on improving your systems, processes and address potential variations early on they will become anomalies that at some point may spiral out of control and become significantly bigger and tougher to manage in the future. Everyone must empower themselves to take control of their own development. As a manager or sales leader, you are more aware of the bigger picture, and thus the responsibility rests on your shoulders to use that knowledge to instigate the progressive change that is needed to support your team's development.

Finding mentors and advocates

As you grow, the need for an experienced and trusted advocate to help you navigate the scenarios that lie ahead becomes increasingly important. A mentor has the expertise to thoughtfully challenge and ask the appropriate questions of you to support your growth, development and future success. Finding and developing a relationship with one or even several individuals that you can openly talk about your experiences with can be invaluable in helping you appreciate your value and the impact that you're making on a consistent basis.

I would advise against relying on a partner or friends as being mentors as they may not have the company, industry, sales or management experience that you need help with. Furthermore, there is sometimes a tendency for bias in the advice that they provide because of their personal relationship with you.

Being honest

If you have an appetite for growth, are ready to ask for help without the fear of judgment and willing to make changes on the back of constructive criticism and advice, you've laid the foundation for an open and honest relationship with your mentor.

A mentor can only help if the mentee is willing and open to receiving advice and knowledge to support their growth. If you decide to listen but seldom implement or experiment with the ideas that the mentor provides, then it will put a strain on your relationship. You need to be honest with both yourself and your mentor throughout the process. The more they can understand about your thought process and level of reasoning, the more that they will be able to help you.

There can sometimes be a fear of judgment when the mentee shares information and experiences with the mentor, but if you've selected the right mentor then this fear will dissipate because of the opportunity to learn and sharing of knowledge that will take place. They will translate each failure or negative experience into a learning opportunity.

What to look for in your mentor

My criteria for a mentor was to look for individuals that I respected, aspired to be like and that challenged my way of thinking. I found that having a combination of mentors that included senior managers, individuals from different departments and even experts from other businesses helped shape a better approach and thinking that supported my hunger for development.

The relationships I built with mentors have been so strong that I remain in touch with them today and feel that I can call on them, at any time, for advice or support. Developing this type of relationship takes a commitment on both sides as well as a mutual respect and culture of providing support without the fear of judgment, allowing for an openness that supports and fosters growth.

Managing frustrations and understanding their origin

I am sure that you can relate to a situation where you've been upset or annoyed because you've been unable to achieve the desired outcome that you were looking for? This lack of progress can sometimes be frustrating and have an impact on our future behaviour and outlook. In order to manage your frustrations, it's important to understand their origin and the catalyst that is the real reason for causing the frustration in the first place.

When you react to a situation and show your frustration it can be perceived in a negative way. You may not have intended for this to happen; however, it's easily done and can influence another person's perception of you. Whilst it's difficult to control, you must try to understand what the root cause of the frustration is that is creating a sense of anger or irritation within you. Whilst you may not be able to control your emotions all the time, it's important to understand whether the frustration is linked to certain situations, individuals or something else entirely.

Frustrations are an opportunity

When developing as a manager it's easy to feel frustrated because there is so much that you're focused on and asking of yourself and your team that sometimes tasks naturally fall by the wayside as they are not considered to be a priority. You may even find yourself asking your team to complete a task, which they fail to do, and as a result your frustrations increase. In this scenario it's easy to let your frustrations take control of you, but what good will getting annoyed do? Will it mean that your team complete the task any quicker?

The better approach, from my experience, is to take a step back and understand why you're frustrated. Is it because you asked your team to do something and they haven't done it, you feel them not completing the task is a lack of respect for you, or because it's meant a deliverable has been delayed, or something else entirely? Once you realise the cause of your frustration you can speak to the individuals to understand why the task wasn't completed and explain the importance accordingly and what the impact of non-conformance potentially is on them, you, the team and other projects.

Every scenario in which you feel frustration is an opportunity to reflect, review and adjust your behaviour to support your continued growth. Whilst some frustrations will be easy to overcome, others will naturally require more time, development of certain skills that you may lack, and most importantly your commitment to yourself. I found that experimenting on managing personal frustrations, like controlling alcohol consumption or my weight, helped develop my ability to overcome work-related challenges. The more frustrations I was able to tackle head on, the deeper my confidence and resolve developed, whilst allowing me to observe and test for myself how to react in different scenarios.

The root cause of your issues

Changing your reaction to frustrations is a hugely important step, and you must acknowledge what is and isn't in your control. If you're frustrated about something that you've had no control over, what can you do about it? Are you able to influence the process in any way? If yes, then go ahead and do that, however you must understand that your role is of an influencer and there is no guarantee that the frustration will go away, and there is a chance that the outcome may be the same. What you need to acknowledge for yourself is that you've tried to change the outcome, but it wasn't in your control.

On the flip side, if the frustration is related to something that *is* in your control then you must do something about it. There is no point getting frustrated time and time again about the same or similar things, especially when it's in your control. You need to be the one to make a change to elicit a different result. Early on in my managerial career I used to get frustrated with staff who didn't complete tasks by the set deadline. As a new manager I wanted people to like me, I wasn't sure how to handle conflict and so I didn't say anything to the team members who weren't completing the tasks, and instead made excuses on their behalf. The longer this carried on, the more frustrated I became, and for the team the behaviour of not competing tasks became acceptable as I had not addressed it.

I realised that my failure to address the root cause of my frustrations meant the issue had started to become chronic and was having a knock-on effect on my ability to manage the team effectively. Individuals on the team thought it was acceptable to miss deadlines because there was no consequence. I slowly addressed the issue by enforcing the deadlines and putting consequences in place for non-conformance. This resulted in me having to have several difficult conversations, which in hindsight would have been avoided had I addressed my frustrations earlier when I first took the role.

Furthermore, it changed the relationship I had with my team at the time. I was no longer a peer and had to adjust my behaviour accordingly to support better management of my frustrations and my growth.

What not addressing your frustrations does

If you care enough about something to get frustrated, then you must also care enough to find a solution for the long term that will help you. If you're not willing to find that solution, then you accept that the frustration will continue to exist and will evolve over time and impact other aspects of your life and career. The longer you let a frustration play out and continue, the harder it becomes to reverse it as habit sets in.

When you don't address frustrations, they begin to control you, your mind and your thought process. You start developing solutions with your frustrations in mind trying to avoid getting yourself in those scenarios and second-guessing outcomes. If you're not ready to address a frustration then acknowledge that you are not ready to do so and understand why that is – maybe because you don't know how, but don't hide behind the sorry excuse and use the word 'can't'. It's like giving up before you've even tried.

Longer term, as frustrations build and you fail to manage them, your mind will start to accept them as a normal response, and soon enough you're not trying to manage one frustration but several of them, which impacts on your thinking and the decisions that you make. Your mind starts looking for a way out and develops solutions that circumnavigate the frustration because it's quicker than dealing with the bigger issues which keep eating up inside.

Changing your mindset and taking control

For growth to be realised, the biggest change that must take place is within you. You must become the master of your own destiny, and if that is to happen you need to change your thinking and take control of your mind and how you've programmed it to respond. Acknowledging this may sound easy, however in practice it requires you to step outside of your comfort zone, embrace the unknown and challenge everything that you currently do and how you do it. It can seem easy to do in one-off situations; however, your success depends on your ability to focus and control your mind whilst realising when negative thoughts are impacting on your thought process, stepping back accordingly and letting your mind settle once again and then taking control.

Sales is a results business and when we don't see the desired outcomes, we tend to start questioning everything around us, which can lead us to defaulting back to our old habits. Once a change process starts from within, it's important to keep it going otherwise any impact will be short lived and you will revert to old habits and thinking.

Impact of conditioning over time

Our exposure over time to certain situations has meant that our behavioural responses have become more frequent and predictable in certain environments or situations as a result of the reinforcement for a desired outcome or response. This conditioning is beneficial to us in some ways but does also have a negative impact too. Rather than thinking things through we're reacting based on the conditioning that we have gone through over time and responding in a uniform manner.

For managers and leaders to realise their potential for growth they need to break free from this conditioning and challenge their own thought process. They need to reassess and create a new cycle of conditioning, which addresses questions differently from when you were a team member without any management or leadership responsibilities.

A child is fearless and doesn't worry about asking a question until they receive a response that they can relate to and understand. However, as they grow older and are exposed to certain environments, they start becoming programmed or conditioned to accept certain answers and norms which unfortunately impact on their growth potential. As an adult, to change this conditioning you must understand your bias and once again become fearless in your pursuit of personal growth and development. This starts with questioning everything and challenging yourself with regard to what you think you know or have been told.

The iceberg illusion

The metaphor that I keep in front of my mind always is of the iceberg. This is a symbolic image that I use on my website too, because when you meet people all they will see is the tip of that iceberg, where you are today and the success that you've achieved. They will probably make judgments about you based on that tip without knowing too much about you, your background or the journey that you've been through which has led to your successes.

It's your responsibility to focus not on what is above the waterline and instead on what's below and that no one sees or feels but you: the hard work, resilience, persistence, discipline, courage, criticism, risks, changes, dedication, passion, honesty, good habits, innovation etc. It is what's below the waterline that will shape you, transform the vision that you see for yourself and that will help you realise your potential. You must ensure that your actions speak louder than words and your commitment doesn't waiver, no matter what challenges are thrown at you.

Chapter 2 Reflection Time

1. How do you cope and manage with change today? What is your process for evaluating the potential impact of the change?
2. Who are your mentors or trusted advisors that you turn to and that help you navigate the situations that you're unfamiliar with or need support on?
3. What are your current frustrations, and more importantly, do you understand their true origin and root cause? How can you tackle these now that you've identified them?

Chapter 3

COMMITTING TO A VISION

Before delving into the more emotive and behavioural themes that are fundamental to growth, it's important to acknowledge and understand whether you're interested or committed to the attainment of the vision that you're working towards. Being interested is simply not enough, and without the required commitment true success is unlikely to be realised. Having a strong vision and being truly committed to it is of paramount importance.

Having an interest, or even being curious, in starting your own business, developing yourself, taking up a new hobby or anything else is an all-important step in the process that leads to commitment. However, for interest to transition into commitment, your mindset needs to shift from something that you would like to do to something that you will do no matter what challenges or barriers you're up against.

I'm sure that we can all relate to having thoughts regarding learning a new language, skill or taking on a challenge that piqued our curiosity. When I reflected on these examples and assessed my thought process, I realised a common theme. If the idea didn't resonate or only interested me, I would often make excuses for why

I might not be able to do something. This was because I hadn't passed the awareness point of where interest turns to commitment. Having acknowledged this, I've reached a point now where rather than making excuses I am honest with myself and those around me, to admit exactly that. It's either not a priority or I need more time to raise my level of awareness towards understanding whether it may become important enough to be committed to.

More recently, I have observed many individuals who have wanted to progress from being a team member, to a manager, to even a sales leader. I have developed my own checklist to validate and assess the individuals who I believe are not just interested but committed to their development and growth:

- They are full of curiosity
- They have a clear vision of themselves and where they want to be
- They see management as the next phase of their development and a stepping stone rather than the peak of where they want to get for monetary gain
- They understand the theory, are comfortable with its application and with adapting it to suit their personality and style of management
- They are honest with themselves about their limitations and ask for help and advice
- They want to use their knowledge, experience and understanding to help others – it's not a kudos thing but an ingrained action to want to help those around you
- They are motivated to realise their potential (not just monetary motivation)
- They have a burning desire to succeed

Whilst this is not an exhaustive list, it helped me qualify whether individuals were looking at roles for the right reasons. On numerous occasions I used this checklist to filter those that liked the idea of managing and to highlight potential situations that they would need to address and tackle if they were truly committed. Those conversations were eye opening for them because they hadn't considered the variety of issues that a manager must deal with on a day to day basis. Management definitely isn't for everyone and requires a level of selfless commitment that puts the needs of their team above everything else.

Identifying with your personal vision

If you're anything like me, you've got a hectic lifestyle both personally and professionally. You're probably inundated with interesting ideas and opportunities that you could get involved in. Before you invest your time, energy and effort it's important to evaluate them in a consistent manner. To do this I would recommend differentiating and assessing your own position between commitment, vision and passion.

These are the three important elements that careful contemplation must be given to prior to making a choice, and for your growth to be maintained. Spending time initially on evaluating these elements will ensure that your decision is grounded and focused towards attainment of your vision with the appropriate level of passion and commitment required.

I've often been asked how I instil these three elements within my teams. It's by no means an easy task and one that requires commitment to growth both on my part and the individuals'. The key starts with understanding the true vision that each person has for themselves. I'm interested in where they want to be in 5, 10 or even 15 years' time, including what they want to be doing, why and how. Once the vision has been established, the individual will have a clear direction they want to go in. I've worked with individuals who have been able to identify their vision in days and for others it's taken significantly longer because they have struggled with the idea of having a personal long-term plan. In some cases, individuals have not believed in this concept and opted not to focus on it; that's their choice, but the difference between those that have a clear vision and those that do not is easily recognisable.

Developing your vision is an opportunity for each person to start seeing things from a different perspective that may not have previously been considered. A perspective that refocuses their mind on what is really important to them versus what they have potentially been spending unnecessary time on. If the vision is a true reflection of the direction that the individual wants to go in then it's easier for them to be committed to activities, opportunities and ideas that will support achievement of their aspirations. The passion will naturally also be there because they realise the long-term benefits obtainable, and rather than considering certain projects as mundane, their mindset shifts and they see them as stepping stones towards attainment of the long-term plan that they have for themselves.

Jake was a new recruit within one of my teams, and as a follow-up from the interview process, I had a conversation with him about his aspirations and personal vision. Jake had taken some time to think about this and identified short- medium- and long-term targets for where he wanted to be. Short term he wanted to establish himself on the team and become a diligent Key Account Manager. In the medium term (five years) he wanted to buy his own home and afford at least one luxury holiday a year. Finally, Jake's long-term vision was to be a manager, and at some point even have his own business.

Identifying with Jake's vision helped me to coach and mentor him towards supporting his growth. When he came to me asking about whether I thought an idea was good or bad, or his actions were justified, I would encourage him to relate it back to his vision and whether it supported achievement of that or the goals that he had set. He quickly realised and started self-assessing ideas and activities in this way and proactively made conscious decisions on whether to take on new projects or not.

Every now and then, Jake, like we all do, needed to talk things through because he couldn't come to a conclusion for himself. In those instances, rather than giving Jake the answer of what I thought he should do, I instead asked him to re-evaluate his vision and to make sure that it hadn't changed based on the progress he had made so far. Once a vision becomes reality it's important to evaluate and reset to ensure that the focus remains, along with the commitment needed.

Developing a commitment to growth

As team members go through different life stages, the only guarantee is that things will change which will challenge them, grow them, and as a result will require them to review and possibly adjust their personal vision, goals and objectives. If they're in a newly formed relationship or decide to get married or are about to have their first child or buy their first house, all these things and more will have an impact on them personally, which could have a knock-on effect on how they react.

Some may see them as distractions from a working perspective, however I see them as critical milestones in each person's development. The hard work (personal and professional) has helped them to reach these milestones. Rather than making assumptions at this stage it's important to support the team members, offer advice if applicable and ask questions to validate any assumptions you are making about them so that you're both able to plan accordingly and together can put the next steps in place to ensure the interest is maintained, at the very least, and commitment continues.

My commitment to my team was always to try and support them and help them grow as individuals. That sometimes meant providing them with exposure to ideas that took them out of their comfort zone. A good example of this is when I organised a mindfulness session for them. A colleague within another team, Lina, practised mindfulness and was keen on becoming a coach. We had a discussion and Lina agreed to host a session for the team. I had heard rumours that some of the senior execs weren't entirely happy with what I was doing; however, I wanted to give my team experiences that would grow them, and as no one raised issues with me directly I wasn't the least bit concerned or intending to change my plans.

When I updated the team on what the plan was for the weekly meeting, some of the team did laugh and joke about what they would be doing, but they appreciated that it was something new and they had nothing to lose. Over time I had broken down many barriers with them and had openly discussed the idea of trying new things, as the experience would help develop them.

During the session they were exposed to chair yoga, mindful colouring and meditation. Most of the team had never experienced anything like it, however the feedback was overwhelmingly positive. They appreciated the concept and could see how it helped relax and focus them. I saw this as a positive, but I wasn't expecting them to rush off and practise mindfulness every day, however I was glad that they were open to the idea of trying new things and experimenting.

I was committed to my team's growth and as a consequence of that I was happy to challenge those around me that felt my actions were not in line with what the company was looking to do. Secondly, and more importantly, teams can get stuck in routines and it can all feel a little too robotic. As the leader who is committed to their growth it becomes your responsibility to cut through the repetitiveness and offer different perspectives that may enhance their thinking and development.

Starting with good intentions

If there is confusion in a person's mind, or they don't have a defined vision, they tend to experiment more and trial different things. It's easy to fall foul and jump on the bandwagon of a good idea that someone has, but you need to consider whether it's important enough to you and whether you will see it through. If you don't take time to do this, at the first sign of a challenge which you're unable to overcome, you will probably quit.

To avoid this situation or where an individual is unsure about their vision or what they want to achieve, it's best to take a step back and take some time out to truly appreciate what it is that they are looking for. Rather than addressing the long-term vision, focus on something that's maybe achievable within 12 months and thereafter focus on the commitment towards that. In following this process, the aim is to encourage that way of thinking and developing a different reflex from what the individual may have been used to.

The impact of peer pressure

Peer pressure can and does on occasion have a significant impact on commitment. It can provide a positive or negative stimulus which impacts on an individual or group of individuals.

Think back, have you ever found yourself pressured into something because friends or other colleagues are doing the same? It's very common especially in large sales team environments. One time there was a bulldozer in the team, Goran, who I worked alongside. Goran was an interesting character. He was a pure hunter who was motivated only by money. He was selfish and only thought about himself and would stop at nothing to get what he wanted. He was considered by many to be rude and unless you had something that benefitted him, he wouldn't acknowledge you or even care that you existed.

Goran was totally committed to what he wanted, however he had never been managed effectively to harness the skills he possessed. He often challenged younger, less experienced members of the team and questioned how they were carrying out their duties and the reason why they were not achieving the results they should be. The younger members of the team looked up to Goran because he was closing deals weekly and they felt pressured to be more like him. They thought that changing their way of working and doing things in the Goran mould would get them better results.

Having different characters and levels of experience within a team is both healthy and conducive to supporting growth. However, there need to be some guidelines developed with regard to the role the experienced individuals play in supporting the less experienced members. The less experienced members are committed to sales, they have ambitions and aspirations to hit the dizzy heights that the more experienced around them have reached, and if they see the bulldozer's actions going unpunished, they will think it's OK to act in that manner too. In my experience, when less experienced members of the team are exposed to this behaviour and nothing happens, their focus starts switching to short-term results from the commitment to long-term development and growth. It's extremely important in these situations to protect the younger members of the team and discuss what the impact of the wrong behaviour will be on the vision that they have identified for themselves.

Those around you must be equally as committed

When you're selecting managers, partners or suppliers to work with you it's important that they are equally as committed to what they do as you are to what you do. If they are not, the likelihood is that you will not receive the level of engagement, service or quality that you are looking for to support your team's growth and desired results.

I don't believe that experience always correlates to the individual having the right level of commitment that is needed. On many occasions I overlooked experienced salespeople in favour of younger individuals with limited experience because I hadn't seen the level of commitment that I was looking for. On one particular occasion, after interviewing several candidates, I offered a manager role to an individual who had the least experience in sales, however he did have more of a varied background and experience within marketing and operations.

It was a calculated risk on my part, and I backed the individual because he had the credentials to do the role along with a strong vision and commitment to his own development as well as the team's. This made him stand out like a beacon from the other candidates. Six months down the line the decision was vindicated because his team were energised, responding to his style of working and delivering results.

When making decisions that will impact the team, it's important to take away the emotion and focus on what's the right thing for them. If you have created a positive environment and culture in the team then it's important not to jeopardise that. There is a responsibility on your part to the team and individuals that will be impacted to recruit a manager who has the right attitude and is committed to their own growth as well as the team's.

Continuous appraisal and learning

I am an advocate of measuring success and believe that it's extremely important that regular appraisals are completed for everyone on the team. Setting goals and regularly checking performance against them, whilst reminding yourself of your vision, keeps your passion alive and ensures you stay on track with the commitment being maintained. An individual with a vision and who is committed will set themselves goals and objectives to work towards and they are more likely to take responsibility for their own progress and development.

Whilst most companies will have a policy of an annual performance review, meeting on a more regular basis to discuss development and continuously adjusting development goals in line with progress that is being made is crucial to continuous growth.

Having said that, I was never a fan of a scheduled weekly one to one meeting. I worked to the premise that as and when issues arose, and individuals needed help, it was the best time to address their concerns and use those situations as learning opportunities. My belief was that in that moment because the desire for them to get to a solution was so strong, they were always more receptive to discussing different strategies and solutions. There was a general rule within the team that promoted the need for thinking through the issue and identifying different solutions before approaching myself or anyone else. However, I always maintained an open-door policy to discuss anything that a member of the team felt they wanted help with or clarification on. Adopting this way of working promoted a commitment to the team where everyone helped one another without the fear of judgment.

Assuming the role

When things are going well, or you have an experienced team that's been together for some time, it can seem easy to manage as there are fewer issues to deal with and your focus is on managing the exceptions. In this situation you need to push and challenge yourself more to grow as there are fewer situations you're proactively being placed in where you're practising your skills, or being asked to react differently from the normal way of working that you have developed.

Developing high-performing teams doesn't just happen, it takes hard work and commitment from you. You learn more in tougher situations and times about yourself and the effectiveness of the skills that you've developed. Your reaction and response to every challenge is a measure of your success.

Some of the best advice that I was given when I was aspiring to transition from a team member to player coach was to assume the role that I wanted. Considering myself as already being in that role whilst constantly thinking about what I would do in each new situation I may find myself in. This approach is interesting because in doing so you start seeing things and thinking about them from a different perspective. You start considering factors that previously you've ignored or not had to worry about, like dealing with communication with other departments or planning for scenarios that aren't just in your personal interest.

I've shared this advice of assuming the role with many individuals who have discussed opportunities for promotions over the years, and a number have stared back at me blankly confused, with their look translating to me asking them to do something which they weren't expecting, especially when there is no guarantee at the end of it. Maybe my unconscious bias kicks in at that moment, but that unwillingness to assume the role says a lot about the person's motivation and commitment. Some of the individuals who have reacted positively to this advice have gone on and flourished in team leader and sales manager roles. If you believe in what you want to do and have that commitment in getting there, you will find a way. If not, you'll find an excuse or someone else to blame!

Picking up the slack

Having developed the environment and a commitment to each person on the team, it's important that when challenges arise your actions speak louder than the words you may have used. Being there for your team and walking the walk by supporting them and picking up the slack shows your desire to do what it takes to help them and the team.

On several occasions, for personal reasons, team members had to take extended periods of time off, which was beyond their control. These are not situations that you can plan for, however your reaction speaks volumes, in terms of how much you care and the value that you place on the commitment that you have made to the individual. Rather than just delegating the responsibility, it's in these unplanned situations where a manager or leader must get involved, get their hands dirty and do what it takes to pick up the necessary slack. Rather than seeing it as an issue, I preferred to see it as an opportunity to validate my knowledge of the sales processes and update myself with subtle shifts and variances that may have taken place in the market. Taking responsibility in this situation enhances your relationship, reputation and proves your commitment further.

Deciding how important it is

Whenever we are faced with a choice, how we react and respond is significant in identifying how important something is to us. You must appreciate that you have a finite capacity, and whilst there are numerous things that land on your desk or in your inbox, you don't have the capacity to get involved in all of them or make them a priority. You must have clarity with regard to what is important to you and prioritise accordingly.

Deciding what is important and what doesn't require your attention can be difficult; however, there are many ways that you can help yourself and improve the process that you take in making the appropriate decision. To help me decide I consider importance based on whether it fits in with my values (more about this in Chapter 4) and what influence, impact or support it provides in my ongoing work towards fulfilling the vision, goals and objectives. If it challenges me, grows me and provides me with a different perspective that I may not have considered, then it's important because it's growing my mind and supporting my development.

Doing it to the best of your ability

Every line manager should want the best for their team and to do things to the best of their ability. To achieve this, it's important to create the right environment and provide them with the appropriate tools and training.

Everyone needs a push from time to time, however an appropriate balance must be struck to ensure we get the best out of the team consistently. A motivated team will over deliver, so focusing on targeting your communication against their vision is likely to generate the deepest connection to the commitment that is needed.

Your capacity to do things

As we grow, experience and responsibility increases, we're promoted into bigger roles and are required to spin more plates than before. This is all great news and fantastic that you're being recognised; however, in order to do the new things that the job demands of you, you must ensure that it's aligned to your vision that you're committed to.

Furthermore, in this situation I've often observed that individuals lose the appetite to maintain certain job tasks, and therefore it's important that you create capacity and delegate some tasks and responsibilities to your managers or team members. Motivation can be lost for a variety of reasons, but more often than not it's because there is no correlation created between the tasks and the vision. The manager needs to communicate how those tasks could benefit their overall long-term vision.

As an example, filing can be considered a boring and mundane task, but if it was communicated by the manager as information management and creating a skill to organise and reference it in a manner where it can be quickly retrieved by the relevant individuals that require access, you're asking the individual to create a solution and showing them why the task is important and needs their attention.

In the same way that you're being given an opportunity to develop, you need to facilitate that development and opportunity for your managers and team. This sharing of responsibilities will potentially support their growth and achievement of their own vision and increase ongoing commitment to the role.

Taking on more doesn't correlate into success. Be mindful about what those tasks give you and whether you can see them through and deliver the quality of output that is needed to enhance your character. If you're interested in taking on something because you believe it will be beneficial to you and have the commitment to see it through, evaluate how you can find the capacity to make it happen.

What can be deprioritised or relinquished from your workload and delegated to someone else? If you've been in sales long enough, you know that something unexpected is always around the corner. You can't plan for it but will have to react to it regardless, which may be a drain on the amount of time you have available. A good strategy to come to terms with the everyday unexpected challenge issue is to block out 30-60 minutes from your day for miscellaneous work that requires your attention. If nothing comes up, then you've got 30-60 minutes back.

Chapter 3 Reflection Time

1. A strong vision, and commitment to that vision, becomes a 'guiding light' for all your decisions. If you're not sure about anything then you can return to your vision and see how it matches against that.
2. How will you evaluate whether your managers, partners or suppliers are equally as committed as you are?
3. If you're looking for a promotion or different role, start assuming the responsibilities to help your appreciation of what the role entails.
4. Delegate tasks to your managers or team members to create capacity for yourself whilst ensuring you clearly communicate and define the correlation to the vision. This will help to maintain their motivation.

Chapter 4

THE IMPACT OF VALUES

Values can be defined as principles or standards of behaviour related to one's judgment of what is important in life. When making decisions (consciously or subconsciously), values help to determine priorities and can act as anchor points or measures to identify if life is turning out the way you want it to. When your behaviour matches the values, you have determined for yourself life is good; however, when you experience behaviours that don't align with your personal values, things naturally don't feel right and you could feel downbeat.

Defining and understanding your values will help you make better conscious choices and decisions. *Example – if you work in a competitive sales environment but don't value competition, the likelihood that you're going to be satisfied in your job will be low.*

As you move through the different stages of your life your values may change. For example, success as a young adult could be measured by getting the degree classification needed to go to university; however, when you start working the success measure could change to money and status. These changes should be embraced because they help you see things from a different perspective. A perspective that you cannot relate to because you've not been in that situation – you may have experienced something similar and you can use that experience to help you, but your interpretation and reaction will be different from someone else's.

Why your values are the key to your personal development and growth

The key to personal growth and development, which supports business growth, is in understanding what your values are and how they are impacting on you.

One of the most interesting and beneficial exercises related to values helped me realise how some aspects of my past, both positive and negative, had resulted in bias forming and impacted on how I assessed the future outlook. It was the first time I had ever completed an exercise like this and in doing so made me realise why I was more inclined to move in certain directions as opposed to others.

To begin the exercise, on a blank piece of paper draw the x axis horizontally across the centre of the page as time in years from left to right and then draw the y axis on the far left of the page running vertically through the x axis. The positive points should be listed on the top half of the page and negative points on the bottom half of the page. Give yourself about an hour to complete this exercise. To start, look back through your life (personal and career) and identify the points when:

1. You were your happiest, what were you doing, who were you with, were there other factors that contributed to your happiness? And now do the same for when you were your saddest or unhappiest or angriest. Map these points on the paper.

2. Now do the same for when you were your proudest, why were you proud, did other people share your pride? Who? Were there other factors that contributed to feelings of pride or ego? And now when you were most ashamed or humiliated, and again map out the points on paper.

3. Finally think about when you were most content, fulfilled or satisfied, what specific need or desire was fulfilled? How and why did your experience give life meaning? What other factors contributed to your feelings of fulfilment? And now when you were dissatisfied, irritated or unfulfilled.

Once you have mapped these points out determine your top 10 values based on the above statements. If you're unclear about words that can be used to describe your values, then search the internet as a number of websites list common personal values that you can refer to.

In completing this reflective exercise, you've started to understand yourself better and key points in your life that may have impacted on the development and changing of your values over time.

The first time I completed this activity and after taking some time to reflect on what I had just learned, three values stood out for me across both positive and negative experiences that I had been through: hard work, honesty and humility. Whilst there were numerous other values that I held and that were important to me, these seemed to be a constant. For me they were important because:

- Hard work is needed to achieve anything that is considered to be important in life. If you remember the iceberg reference in Chapter 2 and the elements that you need to work on within yourself that are below the waterline and not visible.

- Honesty is important for two reasons. Firstly, being honest with yourself at all times and not negotiating with yourself or setting unrealistic expectations of yourself or those around you. And secondly, trust is a cornerstone of building relationships, and when you're committed to doing the right thing and growth then why would you ever want to jeopardise what you've worked so hard to achieve?

- Humility is an acknowledgment that I don't know it all and I'm trying my best but constantly face challenges that may test me and force me to see things from a different perspective from what I am used to. The fact that we're all on our own individual journey means we must treat each other with respect and acknowledge that we're all trying our best based on our experience, understanding and without judgment.

How values change throughout your life

If we accept that change is a constant, we acknowledge that our values will evolve over time too as we grow and develop a better understanding of ourselves. As our experiences shape our thinking, personality and outlook, our values will continue to evolve.

Think about when you started your first job after finishing school, completing college or graduating from university. I cringe at the thought of how naïve I was thinking that I would be able to take what I had learned and simply apply that in a working environment. Theory is great but doesn't take into account many factors like environment, culture, personality, industry and so on. Imagine how far you've come since that time and what experiences you have been through. Each one of those has influenced your thought process and how you react. This process never stops and the more experiences you go through, the more your values will adjust.

One time a member of my team, Dina, was about to go on maternity leave and prior to doing so had assured me that she would be back within nine months at most. Dina was adamant that she wouldn't need the full 12 months and was expecting to come back straight into her role and carry on where she had left off when she returned, within six months. This was the first time I was experiencing someone in my team going on maternity leave and for Dina it was her first child.

Prior to Dina leaving for maternity leave we had mapped out a plan and had recruited cover whilst she would be away. On the advice of the HR team we'd opted for a 12-month maternity cover contract as opposed to the six months that Dina expected to be away. A week or so after Dina's maternity leave commenced, I received a call from her husband to say that she had given birth to a healthy baby boy. It was great news, and everyone was delighted for her, however the delivery was by caesarean section and Dina was in a lot of pain and would need time to recover.

Several weeks after the birth and once things calmed down, Dina and I managed to have a chat. Without any prompt she outright stated that there was no way she would be back within six months. Dina, whilst being very happy, was overwhelmed and the birth of her baby boy had changed her outlook on life. Suddenly, and rightly so, work wasn't a priority, and she had something more important to consider and care about.

A further twist to this tale took place about nine months into Dina's maternity leave when she contacted me to tell me that she'd decided not to return to full-time employment. She wanted to focus on being a mother and take advantage of spending as much time as possible with her son. It was the right thing for Dina because it was important to her, and she wasn't willing to compromise on that.

A year or so later Dina was balancing bringing up a child while trying to set up her own business from home. She'd managed to find a balance where she was able to be there to see her son grow up while starting a business that offered her the flexibility that she needed. The changes that Dina went through meant that certain values became more or less important to her at different stages of her life. The same is true as a result of any significant change that a person goes through.

Knowing what you stand for and what you are willing to accept

Understanding and using your values can provide an excellent way to setting standards for yourself that you can measure against. In doing so it can help you set certain boundaries and create reflex responses to ensure that your values remain intact. I consider knowing and understanding what you stand for is extremely important in business and managing teams because it helps you determine your benchmarks for what you will and won't accept when faced with challenging situations. If your values come into question you will instantaneously feel the need to act, and rather than taking a back seat and doing nothing you will be compelled to address the issue and act accordingly.

It's your responsibility for setting the standards that you want to promote or aspire to achieve and be maintained. At some point in your career to date you may have experienced a meeting where one individual may have been mocked or ridiculed for holding a viewpoint that went against what some of the team believed was an appropriate course of action to take. There will be individuals that remain silent and don't contribute; however, if you're one of those individuals that doesn't believe the reaction of your peers is fair and the behaviour is not appropriate, then you must stand up and address it, otherwise you've accepted a standard that goes against your values.

I am not suggesting that you should endorse the idea that is being questioned, but maybe it hasn't been articulated as well as it could or there is a misunderstanding. Either way, by saying nothing the person being mocked is probably embarrassed and unlikely to share in a similar forum again and could be scarred by the experience, whilst the individuals who were mocking their colleague start thinking their behaviour is acceptable and they continue to exert their influence in the same way at future meetings. If the values that you hold are questioned, then it's important that you address the issue rather than ignoring it, as even doing so once can start the process of a bad habit being formed.

The impact on your behaviour

Having acknowledged and realised your values, it's extremely important that you keep this front of mind and your own behaviour matches the values that you believe in. No one likes to work in an environment or for someone who promotes the do as I say and not as I do culture. In the same way your values impact on your behaviour, they can influence others around you too.

Values are like a subconscious currency that impacts on your behaviour. When you realise what's important to you and you find yourself in a situation where others are displaying behaviours that you don't wish to associate with, you start drawing yourself away from those individuals and slowly stop investing yourself with them. By making this realisation, choosing to move away from the value that you're not attracted to, you're setting a higher standard for yourself. As you understand more about the impact that value has on yourself you will naturally realise how it's linked to other values and behaviours which you may need to adjust.

Making these changes is critical to success. Your behaviour sets the tone for those around you. Will you be judged – yes, that happens whether you do something positive or negative, but it's because you're making changes that everyone can see and because it's important to you and will ultimately improve you as a person, those around you and your team. If you choose not to make behavioural changes or there is a mismatch between your values and the behaviour you display, then the likelihood is that your actions will be erratic and there will be inconsistency in how you manage people, situations and your team. I would encourage you to use your values to help guide your behaviour – it will promote consistency, the setting of boundaries and helping those around you.

The bias in your decision making

I've read numerous articles that suggest that human beings have a natural bias towards negative experiences. Whenever we're in a situation or we want to do something new, our tendency is always to remember those negative moments first rather than the more positive experiences. When you're taking a big decision it's important to recognise the risks and limitations of both positive and negative experiences but then also to understand the benefits and improvements that could be possible if executed in the appropriate manner.

I've always found that acknowledging the negative experiences and using them as a benchmark or case study for how we don't want something to go can help to set better objectives, measures, and it gives the team a greater focus on what to be mindful of. It's likely that since the last experience we related to there would have been further changes in variables, therefore it's important to always assess the new variables that could be making an impact.

For any unconscious bias to be identified in the decision-making process you must learn to understand yourself and realise when and where your unconscious bias is impacting on you. Developing a reflective process where you're able to observe yourself carefully and understand how and why you're reacting the way that you are in certain situations will help identify your limitations and ask you to question your intention and motivation.

I was born in Kenya, but because I moved to England at the age of six, my accent wasn't native and completely formed. I have always found it interesting how a person's accent can create bias, and one time I remember observing a team member, Will, who I thought had an unconscious bias towards individuals with strong foreign accents. In the presence of two members of the team who were both from South East Asia and had strong accents, more often than not Will would lose focus and start fidgeting with his phone, pen or anything else he could lay his hands on.

I knew Will well and he wasn't a racist; however, in conversation with him I learned that he had some learning difficulties which meant that he found it difficult to concentrate and process the accents he wasn't familiar with. By understanding his challenges and explaining this to his two colleagues, they were extremely supportive and were able to provide him with summaries on key points that they were covering so that he could continue to contribute in the meetings.

Unconscious bias has a positive influence too, and at times could be working in your favour. Imagine working in central London every day and using the underground or train for your commute. Your unconscious bias over time kicks in, and without realising you may find yourself entering the train at the same door every morning to provide access to the best exit for your stop when leaving the train, and the same for your return journey back home. In the same way there are numerous activities and actions that we unconsciously perform without thinking about and do so as if we're on autopilot. I've read articles suggesting that this unconscious bias is always present and cannot be switched off, so be careful what you're doing and how you're doing it!

Making conscious decisions

Taking time to recognise and define your values will help in not only making more conscious decisions but allowing you to explore your potential whilst reducing any time where you might negotiate with yourself.

Knowing my core values has helped me enormously in changing the result of situations where in the past I may not have said something which could have easily misled a customer or colleague. Focusing and keeping my values front of mind means that I consciously refuse to take decisions where I am compromising on them. Taking the easy decision and withholding information today might make the problem go away, however it would never sit well with me if it meant I was misleading someone. It does mean that in some situations I have to think carefully about my approach and how I am going to raise a certain issue and talk it through. It focuses me on thinking about the situation from different perspectives, meaning that I don't second guess the issue and remain impartial.

The key thing for me is that I am transparent and my conscience is clear because I am trying to do what I consider to be the right thing.

I remember receiving a complaint about two individuals on my team, Ash and Ed, from the head of the Operations Department, where a member of the operations team was appalled at the trolling and abuse that Ash and Ed were giving to one of their colleagues, Sarah. It was a serious complaint and showed a lack of respect and courtesy towards a fellow colleague, where they were referring to her in a derogatory manner and using bigoted terms of reference towards her. Sarah had not been present during this exchange, however other members of the team were there and could hear the exchange that was taking place. This type of behaviour has no place in society let alone in a dynamic, multicultural office environment.

I spoke to Ash and Ed individually to make them aware of the complaint and get their side of the story. Both independently admitted to making certain comments; however, they were keen to point out that it was just friendly banter amongst them and they meant nothing by it and would never use those terms or phrases when talking to Sarah directly. As always in these situations, the perpetrators didn't realise the impact of their actions, and I had to explain it to them in a language that would make sense and leave no room for interpretation.

I outlined the seriousness of the situation and what would happen if the complaint had been lodged with HR directly or if Sarah was made aware by other colleagues and she raised a complaint. Furthermore, regardless of whether they considered it to be banter or not, it was distasteful and there was no room for that type of behaviour on my team because it went against my values, and I am sure against the values of other teams too.

Luckily for them, no official complaint was made to HR, and whilst Sarah heard about it on the grapevine from her colleagues, she had spoken to me and was happy with the lesson they had been given and didn't want to take matters further.

Taking the complaint seriously sets a standard. Nobody should be able to do the wrong thing and get away with it, but where there is an opportunity for development in helping individuals to understand the impact of their actions, it should be used accordingly, as long as the individuals are willing to learn from their mistakes and adjust their behaviour.

The influence of past experiences

I've recently started consulting for a family business that was established more than 30 years ago and has grown steadily over that time. The sales team have historically been focused on revenue growth, and in order to achieve targets offered discounts to clients on a regular basis. As the markets have shifted, and coupled with an increase in raw materials and labour costs, the business cannot sustain the same level of discounting and has had to increase costs to find a breakeven point. After years of working in a discounting culture to achieve their results, the sales team are now struggling with accepting that discounting is not an option. Furthermore, they are unwilling and have created a mental block within themselves to approach customers and raise the issue with them.

Whilst I accept that it's not an easy conversation to have, the business must change the process of how decisions have been made to have any chance of success. In supporting this challenge, I helped the sales team develop some alternative strategies to take to customers, all of which required an increase in current rates and small volume discounts which could be justified only if certain longer term minimum order targets were met. I helped them understand their conscious bias and manage the new set of objections that they were likely to receive and overcome the barriers from their past, which was stopping them from pushing through price increases.

If you don't address issues from the past and acknowledge them, they could continue to impact on how you take decisions today and into the future. If the issue becomes a subconscious bias and you act on autopilot without understanding the impact, the effect could create a position where orders are running at a loss and the business becomes unsustainable.

What happens when you don't consider the bias?

When you don't consider your bias then decisions can come across as arbitrary, without any rationale, at times ignorant and not understanding the needs of the business, your team or clients. Imagine when you're having a conversation with a prospect and they raise an objection which you believe you've heard several times before – your subconscious bias automatically has a response. However, it may not be appropriate for this prospect because what they do is subtly different, and you may have misinterpreted things.

Everyone needs to be mindful of this subconscious bias, acknowledge it's there and listen, observe and ask further clarification questions to allow the prospect to explain why, as opposed to assuming you know the answer.

Knowing yourself and what you stand for

Understanding yourself and being comfortable with who you are and why you're thinking and operating in the way that you do is extremely important for you, your team and your future success. Recognise that you're in the position you are because of your hard work, dedication and commitment. When you appreciate the impact of your values and understand what they truly mean to you, you make better decisions, quicker and can react to situations with a deft assurance.

You could compare this to confidence, but it's not the same. You can be confident but lack the depth of understanding and come across as arrogant. However, when you know yourself on a deep emotional level you understand and appreciate why you react in a particular way, the bias that impacts your decision making and how best to approach situations in a manner that complements the values you hold. Knowing yourself better than anyone is vital, especially in challenging situations when there is significant pressure and small margins at play between success and failure. If you don't understand yourself and are swayed by those around you, then the likelihood is that you're making decisions that you may not be in complete agreement with and which could contradict your values and beliefs.

Don't let anyone take advantage of you

When you don't believe in yourself or there is a lack of conviction within you about who you are and what you stand for, you can open yourself up for others to take advantage of you. Whilst you may not realise it at the time, it can lead to manipulation and a knock-on consequence that could have a more damaging impact if not addressed.

Working in sales means we're surrounded by incredibly persuasive individuals who have developed the tools to convince us why certain decisions, which in their opinion would be the right thing to do, are justified. However, accepting my values and appreciating what I stand for has meant that I am not easily swayed or willing to take decisions when I am not in complete agreement or don't believe I have enough information to hand. Our persuasive colleagues are excellent at what they do and can cause an element of doubt to form in your mind; however, when you give yourself some time to reflect, you're able to see through the argument and contextualise why you're making a certain decision.

Whilst I would love to say that no one has ever taken advantage of me, it's happened on more than one occasion, but it's something that everyone needs to go through to realise the impact it has and how you need to adjust your behaviour and actions to ensure that it doesn't continue to happen.

One specific individual from early on in my career, Sharon, springs to mind when I am contemplating this topic. She would use her position of authority to try and influence the outcome and push me, and others around me, to move in a direction that I was uncomfortable and not in complete agreement with. Sharon had significantly more experience at the time, both from a business and industry perspective, and I found it very difficult to say no, even when I disagreed, because she always had a perfect response and persuasive argument. As an example, Sharon wanted sales teams to position certain product developments in a specific way which significantly exaggerated the product's capability. I was against doing this, but succumbed to her influence because of how well she delivered her argument and pushed the onus on me being seen as a barrier to the company achieving its sales targets.

On this occasion I accepted it because I thought maybe I don't understand things as well as Sharon does and was fearful of being labelled as the reason why sales targets had not been achieved. However, when I was in the same situation with her again on another similar topic, I felt as though it was déjà vu and I was being manipulated. It was an uncomfortable feeling and it didn't sit right with me. The experience did create a challenge for me in that I lost respect for Sharon and wasn't willing to accept anything that she proposed in the future without making my own assessment. I had watched the previous experience play out and her short-term strategy had meant we achieved our sales targets, but the problems were building in other areas which would need to be managed.

I can't blame Sharon for me accepting something that I didn't agree with; that was a failure on my part entirely. However, the experience taught me an important lesson to never accept something that goes against my values. Losing respect for Sharon meant that I didn't know how to react to her and for some time I chose to avoid her because I didn't want to get myself into a conversation with her. It was me running from a problem and unfortunately you can't keep doing that in business. I only got over this issue when in a future situation I didn't succumb to Sharon's pressure and stood my ground. A small victory, but one that meant I could move forward and learn from the error of my ways!

Being honest with yourself

We all go through moments of discontent and disillusionment. In those moments when you're down and need to pick yourself back up and move forward, you can't always rely on others and need to be honest with yourself and learn to pick yourself up and get your head back in the game. Everyone is going through their own challenges both from a personal and professional context. The person you need to be honest with throughout is yourself.

The simple reality is you can't rely on anyone except for yourself to execute and achieve your vision for yourself. It's not your best friend's or colleague's vision, it's yours and you're responsible for setting the benchmarks, tests and assessments to ensure you're constantly working towards achieving it.

No matter what, if you are honest with yourself you create that space to allow yourself to make mistakes, not judge and subsequently grow and accept yourself. You'll also find that your outlook on those around you changes. How you talk to them and coach them will transform. Ultimately, the only thing that you have control over is yourself and your actions, so the more honest you are, the healthier you will feel, and better the decisions you will make for yourself and your future.

Finding shared values

For any business or team to be successful, there will be a set of shared values that become the anchor point for cooperation. These shared values are what brings your business partners, suppliers or team members together, and will keep everyone focused on the task at hand or achieving the joint objectives.

You may have a host of different personalities; however, the shared values are what has been accepted as defining a form of commonality within the team. In my teams I used to openly talk and focus on two shared values: hard work and honesty. These are two of my three core values and because they were important to me, I used these as building blocks in determining the team's values.

My rationale for using these two values was that hard work was needed to achieve success and the objectives that had been set, whilst everyone on the team needs to be contributing towards the numerical targets and softer subjective goals. Without honesty as a team, we would not be able to trust one another and make decisions that would support our progress and development. By creating an environment where the team were able to speak openly about mistakes and have no fear of being judged, we were all able to use each other's experiences to support one another as well as find creative solutions to challenges that came up. We all made mistakes, however there was no blame culture and instead each instance was an opportunity to learn collectively as the likelihood was that if one person was experiencing something there was a chance that others would find themselves in similar situations too.

The basis on which cooperation is formed

By finding common shared values, businesses and teams move forward together and communicate with one another more effectively. There will still be disagreements from time to time and differences of opinion that need to be considered and analysed. However, there is a mutual respect and trust with one another which fosters a mode of cooperation where issues are discussed openly, and solutions sought collectively that are in the best interests of all concerned.

In Yuval Harari's book titled *A Brief History of Humankind*, he makes an interesting observation with regard to why human beings are the most successful species on earth and attributes their success over other animal species to the ability to cooperate more effectively.

It's no surprise that creating a system that encourages cooperation and where communication flows are such important ingredients for success. Without this cooperation, issues are rarely resolved, and teams are unable to move forward effectively.

Building a shared team foundation for growth

The shared values are not just important for results. They are important in shaping the bond within a team. When you conduct business with your core values front and centre, there is a different feeling you generate from the results that are achieved. It's confirmation that what you believe in and are working towards is possible, and you don't have to do things in a manner where your values come into question. Additionally, your team, because of the inclusive process that you have adopted, feel part of the success and are aligned with you.

Disengagement and a lack of togetherness

I've seen the other side of not having shared values in a team, which can still lead to quantitative targets being achieved; however, there is a lack of togetherness and consistency in approach and execution of results. A manager within another team, Jorge, was a pure hunter, and only interested in hitting the numbers at any cost whilst not placing enough importance on the softer side of the role. Jorge's team were programmed and focused on closing new business and weren't engaged with one another as a team. They rarely met to share ideas and instead worked autonomously and concentrated on individual gain. This strategy is great when you need to grow quickly and increase market share in a new territory or capitalise on a new product launch, but it can have a detrimental impact longer term.

At some point the initial growth will slow, and without having shared values and a vision, each person on the team continues to operate as an individual and independent from the rest of the salesforce. If they worked together collectively and hunted in packs with a common strategy, they would have a better chance of success and could take advantage of the lower hanging fruit within the market.

Whilst I'm using this story to explain the impact of not having shared values, it's important to note that Jorge is doing what he believes to be right to deliver the results based on the objectives that have been set. If those are achieved at the expense of shared values then maybe that is acceptable to him, his team and department manager; however, from my perspective I have always preferred to focus on collective growth that is sustainable and which provides consistent future revenue within the boundaries of any servicing that is required.

Chapter 4 Reflection Time

1. Complete the values exercise to understand how aspects of your life, both positive and negative, have led to bias forming and how this has impacted on your outlook. What values have you identified that resonate with you?

2. Can you identify with any specific examples of bias in your decision-making process? What are your plans to address this?

3. What are your team's shared values to support cooperation and growth?

Chapter 5

CONTEMPLATING THE PERSPECTIVES

I attribute a large part of my growth and continued success to having developed the ability to acknowledge and understand things from multiple perspectives to what I would consider to be my default. Developing this ability has reduced the amount of assumptions I make when assessing opportunities, modelling out scenarios and taking decisions.

Whilst human beings can consider different perspectives, they lack the ability, and capacity, to consider all the perspectives that are available in each situation. Knowing this, what we can do is work on developing ourselves to look at things from as many perspectives as we are able to process to reduce the volume of assumptions we make.

In order to improve your appreciation of the different perspectives available, you must change your approach and be ruthless with your own thinking and how you manage your own bias. Over time I challenged myself to better understand different viewpoints, and to help with this I addressed one key reaction that I observed within myself: I found myself using the term 'I think' frequently in conversations with my team and those around me. When I thought about it more, I understood that in those moments I didn't actually know the answer and was making assumptions that felt right, based on my bias and emotions at that moment. To stop myself from doing this I adjusted my behaviour so that whenever I found myself about to use the term 'I think', I stopped myself and instead asked more questions so that I could understand the subject in more detail and from alternative perspectives available.

In adjusting my behaviour and following this simple process meant that I began researching the questions that I didn't know the answer to in order to acknowledge those previously ignored perspectives. Additionally, I found myself asking more direct questions of those around me, and especially those whom I considered to be experts or had a better understanding of certain topics. Changing my approach and reflex meant that not only did my awareness improve but so did my ability to design better solutions and propositions. I still make assumptions; however, I also try to ask many more questions so that I have a greater context and understanding.

Evaluating opinions and their significance

When you start considering more of the perspectives that exist, you create room for improvement and start becoming more open to other ideas that may exist and differ from your own thinking. Over time, and as your ability to appreciate a greater range of perspectives improves, you start being able to identify common themes which will allow you to design better processes and build better solutions which you'll be able to articulate in a more inclusive manner.

Given the infinite number of opinions and considerations that need to be made, it's important to accept that in any situation or circumstance the likelihood is that you'll only ever be able to understand, appreciate and mentally process a handful at most. It's because of this that you need to continuously be open to acknowledging new perspectives that you may not have considered previously. As your experience and understanding improves, and the more exposure you have to different situations, the greater the number of perspectives that you may be able to appreciate and process. Programming yourself to do this will help you develop more robust and sustainable solutions that are built to last with consideration of more than just the factors that you consider to be important. Furthermore, the planning process will be more considered and robust.

In any given situation, several strategies can be implemented to solve the same issue; however, the key to success is based on continuous assessment, review and adjustment of the operational tactics as needed and as variables change. Therefore, the more perspectives you're able to consider upfront, the better your planning will be on how to address the impact of those variables.

The impact of not considering the options

When you don't consider other perspectives apart from your own, the output you present or solution you create is unlikely to be representative or take into account the wider needs of your team or the business. No matter what your level of experience, new variables are always at play that need to be reviewed before making a decision.

By not involving or considering other perspectives you're failing to grow your own thinking, developing limitations and creating bias, which will result in an output from a limited viewpoint and one that may not resonate with the vast majority within your team or even the business. This failure to consider differing viewpoints can also lead to a greater number of objections being raised, which could delay planned initiatives from being launched.

My early grounding in process management resulted in a default-like response where I always veered towards procedure whenever I was faced with any challenges or objections being raised against me or an idea I was proposing. Whilst this provided me with some comfort, I was failing to see the perspectives of those around me and what the process did not consider or where it was not designed adequately enough. When I first took on team management responsibilities, this bias towards process continued and I would often use that as my fallback rather than considering the needs of others. What happened over time was that processes would fail because the team didn't follow them as a result of my failure to consider their views and new variables that were at play, like the different ways of working as a result of the evolution of technology. I used this experience to change my approach and began considering the needs of my team, assessing it as part of my criteria prior to making any decisions.

How important is experience?

The more experience you gain can lead you to think that you're capable of considering different perspectives independently and without the need to involve others prior to making decisions. However, the views and needs of those around you will constantly change based on their experience, and as a result it's extremely important to always request their input as opposed to second guessing what you think you know.

Imagine yourself having an argument with a friend, colleague, or anyone else for that matter. You believe that you're right based on the information and knowledge that you hold, and the other person thinks the same based on their experience and knowledge. So, in this scenario how many perspectives do you think exist and who's right and who's wrong? Because there are two people it's easy to think that there are two perspectives; however, in truth there are infinite perspectives available. Our minds have a limited capacity to process them all and we make ourselves believe that what we haven't thought about isn't important or relevant, but that is just our limitation and lack of understanding the impact. Depending on the perspective and your level of understanding, there are varying degrees of truth.

It's never black or white

Knowing and understanding the various perspectives that have been considered has also led me to conclude that things are never black or white, there is always a grey area. This grey area is actually very important because it confirms the existence of unknown variables or doubt. The grey area makes planning a challenge, however it can often also create opportunities that were previously not considered or apparent.

I used to have regular discussions with a finance director, Henry, about what the process should be for customers that hadn't paid their invoices on time. He believed the credit controller in his team was well within her right to issue legal proceedings once an invoice had not been paid and wanted the relevant account contact in my team to have that conversation with the client. I had an issue with this because I saw this as a finance-related issue and nothing to do with client servicing. The finance team had the details for the accounts payable team from the completed order form, so I felt the credit controller should contact the customer's accounts payable team directly and discuss the issue.

Henry wanted my team to manage it because he didn't have the resource and he saw it as a customer issue and my team's responsibility. We were at an impasse and found ourselves in this grey area where we could appreciate each other's point of view but didn't agree with the respective arguments that we were tabling. Whenever cash flow became an issue, we would have the same conversation and restate our position to one another. To support best practice, I did work with my team to adjust the process to make it mandatory to collect specific information like the purchase orders which would help the finance team; however, this was to ensure that Henry could not use that as an excuse.

Whilst I was happy to stand up for my team and fight their corner, these conversations are draining and do not help the business overall. My belief is always to focus on fixing the root cause of the issues as opposed to skirting round it. Henry and I are friends, we respect one another but do always laugh about this because we both know that neither one of us was ever going to move out of the grey area in relation to this topic. The ideal solution, from my perspective, would have been to increase headcount within the finance team, whereas Henry, from his perspective, wanted to add this item to the long list of things that the customer service team was already responsible for!

Having a diverse network that challenges you

Successful individuals and businesses need diverse networks that offer an alternative perspective and one which challenges your thinking. The more diverse your network, the more vigorously thought through the conclusions that you will be able to develop, which will ultimately support growth.

When you have a group of diverse individuals with freedom of thought and expression, how you communicate with them, ask for help and support is crucial for your continued growth. We live in a society where we are surrounded by experts, and the complexities of the various industries that exist make it extremely difficult to understand each nuance. These diverse individuals are a kind of expert who can help you navigate maybe the technical jargon or provide an opinion on a subject that may enhance your thinking or challenge your current thought process.

I often talk to my niece and nephews about some of my business challenges. I find that children have an excellent way of telling you straight out whether something makes sense or if it's too complicated and full of waffle. Whereas in the past I used to fear asking for help or advice because I viewed it as a weakness, now however, talking to different individuals and taking their views into account whilst challenging my own assumptions has become a significant strength and allowed me to grow.

Surround yourself with people that will grow you

It can be extremely scary to have people question you and challenge you, but if you're able to get yourself to understand the benefits it brings and how it can help you, then you'll quickly see progress in your development as well as those around you.

A good example of this is when you're recruiting people to work with you or within your team. I am an advocate, depending on the role, of identifying individuals that bring something different to the team outside of the core competencies that are required. Identifying individuals with complementary skills to yours or others in the team supports growth and development, as well as pushing the boundaries that may have been created. In London and within most large western cities we're fortunate to have the opportunity to work with diverse groups. This exposure helps us understand different cultures and provides invaluable context, which supports the ongoing appreciation of differences that exist.

Appreciating different views

As you learn to consider more diverse opinions and perspectives, naturally you'll come to your own conclusions and determine which ones you agree with versus others that you cannot relate to. Regardless of whether you agree with them or not, it's important to appreciate the different views, as at some point they could become relevant and provide the context that you need. Even as you appreciate certain perspectives over others, this is based on your knowledge and understanding and does not mean what you cannot relate to is incorrect. It's better to see it as an idea that you haven't been sold on just yet and need more convincing.

In many businesses, the higher you reach, the greater the impact of business politics becomes. I detest politics or the games that are played, however there was an important lesson I learned that politicians are great at. Irrespective of whether they agree with your viewpoint or not, they will always acknowledge and appreciate your position on a topic. Them knowing your perspective probably won't change their mind, and they handle those situations by deflecting the argument and objections that have been raised.

Criticising is the easiest thing to do

I would be a hypocrite if I suggested that I haven't criticised anyone. It is sometimes the easiest thing to do when we don't appreciate their perspective or realise the rationale that they went through to come to whatever conclusion they have, especially when we might have a different solution in mind. Given we are limited in how many perspectives and opinions we can consider, I now prefer to think with a more open mind, where I recognise that individuals are trying their best. However, sometimes and for whatever reason, they may not have completely thought their idea through or appreciated the impact of their decision or proposal.

The next time you find yourself in a situation where you're about to criticise someone, ask yourself how it felt when you were in a similar position and individuals didn't ask you to explain your rationale or thought process. Rather than criticising and offering no solution, change your approach and ask a question instead to understand the logic and rationale to appreciate how the individual has come to that conclusion.

Creating a reflex to investigate

If you agree that you don't know it all then you must develop a reflex and mindset to continuously learn and ask questions. Whenever you're in a situation where you're going into a meeting where the topic is not familiar, read up on it before the meeting or ask someone within your network or team to give you some context. This simple yet effective approach will mean you're engaged during the meeting and will be able to ask constructive open questions. You must create a reflex where you're not waiting for things to happen but are taking control of your own development and learning.

Furthermore, these instances are great for promoting the experience and knowledge of others within your team and boosting their brand, which supports their continuous growth too.

The biggest battle is in your head

We live in a time where mental health issues are now being talked about more openly, which is a positive step. There is nothing wrong with asking for help or recognising that you're unsure and need support and direction. We are all collectively responsible for creating an environment that fosters inclusiveness and where individuals feel comfortable with asking for help without the fear of judgment.

At the beginning of my career I worked in an environment which was very male dominated, where you were belittled for not following in the footsteps of senior folk within the business. The culture was toxic, and you weren't paid to think and instead were required to complete tasks in a uniform manner without offering any opinions or engaging with those around you. This type of negative environment felt uncomfortable and unnatural to me and made me fearful of asking even the simplest of questions because I had no idea as to how it would be received or what the response back would be. Needless to say, I didn't stay in that environment long and opted to leave and maintain my sanity rather than remaining in a dictator-like culture.

I consider myself to be fortunate that I've had some exceptional managers and close colleagues with whom I've developed excellent working relationships. The mutual respect and willingness to support one another has allowed us to share ideas and talk about issues openly. These relationships have helped me validate my thinking on occasions when I've doubted myself and given me confidence to ask questions whenever I've needed clarification. We all go through moments of doubt, and having people to talk to and support us helps us categorise, prioritise and create distinctions that are aligned to our values. Without this basic recognition, issues can build within you and soon enough they can overwhelm you and take control of your mind.

Take a step back before taking a decision

Pressure can have both a positive and negative impact. You need to recognise the signs, and when it's impacting you adversely take a step back. If your mind is full of doubt, take some time out, verify, validate and then decide what the best course of action is. In a fast-paced sales environment it's important to be nimble and react quickly, however you must make decisions with clarity of mind and focus.

When I was under pressure or needed to make a decision in an edgy environment, I would typically ask three key questions of myself:

1. Who was going to be impacted by the decision?
2. What were the risks involved?
3. What were the rewards or possible outcomes?

Asking these three questions bought me some time, but also made sure that I wasn't making an arbitrary decision based on emotion and instead went back to my objectives to understand the potential impact. Where possible, I would involve others in the decision-making process too and use those instances to brainstorm ideas if needed. Whilst I was capable of analysing the information and taking the decision, I found these were excellent opportunities to coach the team and help them manage the process which no doubt they would be responsible for in the future.

Seeking validation

Asking a question when you feel that you should know the answer can create panic and doubt, but this should in no way be a reason for you not to ask. If you're unsure for whatever reason, if it's making you feel uncomfortable then you must ask the question, no matter how you feel.

One time I remember a colleague, Lucy, was asking several questions that normally she would have known the answers to and managed with her eyes closed. I was surprised by the questions, however helped her as I normally would. When I saw a pattern of similar situations arising, I became a little concerned as it was uncharacteristic for Lucy, who was a very confident individual. Rather than making any assumptions, I spoke to a close colleague about my observations who had noticed a difference too.

Having had my concerns validated, I caught up with Lucy and asked her if she was OK. She clearly wasn't. She broke down and described issues at home that she was going through which were playing on her mind and challenging her confidence. I offered my support and further help whilst reassuring her to continue asking any questions she felt she needed to because it was an opportunity for her to share rather than keeping things inside. A few days later, things were back to normal with Lucy and she was herself again. She had addressed the issues at home and in doing so her confidence had returned.

If you spend hours procrastinating on the same issue, whilst you might consider numerous ideas and perspectives it can sometimes be a waste of time. There comes a point when you have to seek that validation and ask for help. Rather than letting the task at hand consume you, use it as an opportunity to test yourself, learn more about yourself and reflect on how you reacted to the situations and what you could have done differently. If Lucy hadn't asked for help and instead procrastinated on whether to ask the question, it would have created more doubt over time which could have impacted on her in different ways.

This example is an important lesson in always respecting how your team members' home life situation and issues might affect their work, and how offering that flexibility goes a long way. On that point there are no guidelines set regarding when or how much flexibility should be offered; however, over time I've found myself being more flexible with individuals. My thinking on this has evolved, and through developing relationships with the team you're able to appreciate the impact a home issue can possibly have. If it is impacting on them personally then it's likely to have a negative effect on their work, and the sooner they're able to work through the personal challenges, the quicker they will be able to refocus. Each situation needs to be assessed on its own merits, but proactively offering flexibility is a key management tool that is undervalued and underutilised.

Shifting your mindset

If you keep doing the same things, you're unlikely to see different results from what you have previously experienced. In most instances the biggest barrier to growth will be how you react and do things. To support your growth you may need to consider unlearning some of the things you've done historically and retraining yourself. If your natural outlook is always to focus on the negatives, then you need to shift your thinking and start thinking about the positives. Rather than worrying about the negative things that could happen in each situation, start thinking about the positive outcomes and opportunities that could be created.

I appreciate how easy it is to write this and so many articles say the same thing; however, many individuals are unable to see this through and adjust their thinking and mindset. This is because starting is easy but staying the course through the challenging times and moments of doubt is where individuals lose focus or default back to their old ways of thinking. To succeed in changing your mindset you have to start small and take control of your mind rather than letting it control you. Even when you feel low or a negative thought enters your mind, process it, acknowledge it but choose a positive affirmation as a counterbalance. It's important to condition your mind to always see the opportunity which will expand your thinking rather than the negative which contracts your mind and ability to see beyond the doubt that has been created.

When you allow yourself to create a positive mindset and focus on opportunities, your growth accelerates and pushes you forward at a faster pace. Maintaining positivity in each scenario and at every turn is challenging to do, but the reward is a euphoric sensation where you start to realise that everything happens for the best or leads to a better and bigger opportunity.

Chapter 5 Reflection Time

1. How many perspectives do you consider before making a judgment or taking a decision? What changes will you make to reduce the number of assumptions that you're making? Consider the questions that you need to ask instead in those situations.

2. Can you identify the 'grey area' within projects that you're working on? How can you use this to create opportunities?

3. How diverse is your network? What plans can you implement to develop an environment where diversity is celebrated and individuals are happy to challenge one another?

4. What changes will you consider to better understand your barriers to growth? Is your mindset focused on growth or do you need support to adjust your approach in situations?

Chapter 6

THE IMPACT OF HABITS

It's no surprise that successful businesses and individuals are better at forming more positive habits that provide effective and measurable results. A key reason for this is that they are prepared to constantly evaluate their actions and behaviour, and if needed adjust their habits accordingly to support the change for the desired results to be achieved.

A habit can be defined as a routine behaviour that is repeated regularly and often tends to be subconscious. A habit can impact your thinking, willingness and feelings because of past experiences that the mind has recorded and held on to. In some cases, the person exhibiting the behaviour will not even realise the habit that they are displaying, and it can go unnoticed. This is partly because once a habit is formed we do not tend to self-assess ourselves when performing these routine-like tasks.

When I realised the impact that these subconscious habits have and how long they can take to form and change, I began to recognise their impact on my personal growth goals as well as those around me. I didn't understand the theory, but through my self-reflection practice I was able to observe my automatic reaction in certain situations, which more often than not resulted in a similar instinctive response from those around me. Observing this impact opened my eyes to realising that I needed to change my own habits before I could ask those around me to consider changes and seeing things from a different perspective. The reason why I wanted to make the change and the benefits that I visualised were my motivation. The why is so important.

I was excited when I first noticed the impact of these habits and gave myself a pat on the back for identifying barriers which were impacting my growth. However, when it came to implementing the necessary changes and forming new habits, I realised that it wasn't going to be easy. Knowing what you need to change and physically or mentally making that change can be a challenging and time-consuming process.

I started to research the topic and looked at psychology and scientific studies to help improve my understanding. I thought that 21 days was all you needed to make a habit stick. Through researching the topic, I realised that this wasn't necessarily the case and was the number quoted and used by many, from research studies that had been misinterpreted.

From reading various news articles on the web I came across a summary of a study that was conducted in 2009 by Phillippa Lally, a health psychology researcher at University College London (UCL). The research found that it took on average 66 days for a new habit to be ingrained, and the harder work the habit was considered to be, the longer it would take to form. The research also found that some habits took as long as 254 days to be ingrained with the shortest being 18 days. The 21-day theory originated from a study by Maxwell Maltz who wrote a book in the 1960s in which he claimed that it commonly took 21 days for individuals to get used to something new. This was misinterpreted and became the 21-day theory which was used to motivate people to help them make a start towards any change they were considering.

The key when you're trying to adopt a new behaviour is to acknowledge that it may not be easy, and to achieve the outcome will require focus and commitment. As we've covered in Chapter 3, if it's important enough then you will find a way of doing it, otherwise there will be an excuse that you find and hold on to which stalls your progress. Changing past behaviours and forming new habits is hard work, draining and time consuming, which is why it's not surprising that so many people often don't see it through. However, rather than just thinking about changing old habits, it's crucial to use this insight to ensure that you and your teams form the right habits towards managing key tasks and processes that will influence and impact on your future success.

The reason for wanting to change a habit

The key for creating a new habit or changing an existing one lies in understanding the reasons as to why you're really doing it. Whether it's a change that will impact you personally or professionally, we all start with the right intentions and see something beneficial for us. What we fail to do is think the process through and plan it out. If you make an impulse decision in the evening to stop eating chocolate from the next day, you may start to have second thoughts by the time the sun rises in the morning. It's important to think the change through, plan and create a strategy that you feel will work for you, and most importantly understand how strong your willpower is in maintaining your commitment to do this. If there is a lack of planning or willpower, there will more than likely be a distortion that happens along the way, which leads to defaulting back to old habits.

A good example which many people can relate to is with regard to losing weight, eating healthily or reducing your alcohol intake. It's fairly easy to do any of these activities and achieve short-term results, but if you don't have a longer-term strategy and plan you may lose focus, and the benefits you gained will be reversed quickly.

I made a conscious choice to reduce my refined sugar intake a couple of years ago. It wasn't something that I just dreamt up, I had read lots of articles about the impact that refined sugar had on health and your ability to concentrate and thought that making the change would be positive for me.

I was drinking fizzy drinks and snacking on sugary foods regularly throughout the day, which I wanted to control and limit my intake of. To help me I started by maintaining a food diary, which was eye opening because I realised how much food I was consuming with refined sugar. I then started thinking about what I could substitute the refined sugar products with: as an example, fizzy drinks could be substituted for sparkling water. I also spoke to my network and got ideas from others who had made similar changes to get their advice on what strategies they had used and the challenges that they came across. After a couple of weeks of mentally preparing myself for the change I slowly started removing selected items and replacing them with the substitute products.

Over the course of two to three months I managed to remove most of the refined sugar products. Another part of my strategy to maintain this new habit was to stop purchasing any of the items I didn't want to consume as part of my weekly shop. Whilst it was a simple enough task, the process to change the habit took several months and required more than just the thought of wanting to do it. I'm still off most refined sugar, however I will happily have the odd treat.

My experience of forming new habits has taught me that the better your understanding of the reasons to adopt the new practice, embracing the potential outcomes whilst creating a robust plan and strategy will increase your chances of success.

What made you want to create or start a new habit?

The desire and commitment to improve yourself are extremely important when you want to start a new habit or change an existing one. If you are committed to your personal growth and want to lead by example, then you must recognise the changes you need to make before asking anyone else to change.

If you're focused on self-reflection, analysis and continuous improvement, and should an opportunity present itself to implement positive changes through creation of new habits or by tweaking of existing ones, it's imperative to recognise the changes and thereafter develop a strategy and plan for implementation. This focus on improvement is a contagious habit and a huge motivator personally.

I've often observed individuals and admired habits and practices that they follow and have been keen to understand what draws them to those positive habits. Whilst I would love to implement all the habits, it can be challenging and hence I only do so when I feel ready to make the change. Standing still and not evolving is simply not an option as I'm too curious and have a strong desire and craving for continued growth and development.

What are you trying to achieve and what is your objective?

With any business objective we have a target in mind and it should be no different when you're trying to form a new habit or adjusting an existing one. As part of your planning process some consideration should be given to how you will measure and monitor results.

When I used to give feedback to team members during periodic performance appraisals I always used to start with positive statements and then use the word 'but' before providing a list of things that could be improved on. I hadn't really thought about the impact of the feedback until I went on a training course and the trainer, Nick, explained the negative connotations with using the word 'but' in giving feedback. Nick suggested that in this scenario where the manager is providing feedback, the employee has conditioned themselves to only remember what the manager says after the 'but' and none of the positive elements mentioned before.

Nick's recommendation was to replace the word 'but' with 'and' and restructure the sentence accordingly. The next time I was about to give feedback, I prepared myself as per my plan and wrote a script with AND highlighted and underlined several times. I started the conversation as I normally would, providing positive statements first and then used 'and' instead of 'but' to start the next phase of the feedback, following it up with "…and if you apply yourself in the same way, I have no doubt that you will be able to overcome some of the challenges you have had."

I was shocked at the reaction of the staff member. Nick was right, and they really were waiting for the 'but'; however, when the employee didn't hear the word they were fearing, they actually asked me to repeat what I had just said. I had a similar reaction with several other team members too, which confirmed that the approach was more effective. Seeing the impact made this small change easy to implement and retain!

What happens if you do nothing?

If you are aware of a habit that is impacting on you negatively and do not implement the necessary changes to adjust your behaviour, this could have a knock-on impact on those around you as well as potentially leading to other challenges for yourself. It's not always easy to realise the impact of habits. However, they tend to create a layering effect where other known habits that could and should be adjusted become too deep-rooted, and over time, because of their connection to other habits, become difficult to reverse.

I've observed many senior executives within different companies who I feel have accepted their position and status to be as high as they can reach within their current organisation. When this happens, rather than focusing on continuous improvement and growth, they become reactive in their approach, are typically slower to respond and don't have the same enthusiasm and motivation that they once did. The knock-on result is a change in commitment to the business and growth, but more importantly the team they are responsible for suffers the most.

I cannot say for certain whether this is a true representation and am sure that there will be other factors that I have not considered. However, the fact is that as soon as you're aware of habits that are impacting performance and fail to act, you've accepted a lower standard for yourself, which potentially impacts those around you too.

Investing your time

Like with many things, when you start doing something differently there is either apprehension or excitement because of the newness associated with the activity. Starting or trying to change any habit can be easy because you have the focus, but without the long-term investment of your time and the commitment needed, there is a strong chance whatever you're trying to do won't be maintained.

Time is the one thing that nobody can buy, and as a result it's important to be smart about what you're investing your time in and ensuring that you're getting the results that you expected. It's because we cannot buy time that you must complete the appropriate due diligence and mentally prepare yourself, otherwise you'll start something and then potentially waste time that you could have utilised on other activities, which may have had a greater chance of success.

There is no right time, but don't procrastinate

There is never a right time to start the process of changing a habit; however, the longer you procrastinate, the more chance of finding excuses or other challenges becoming a bigger priority. Once you have recognised the need to change a habit and have done the necessary planning and due diligence it's important to set milestones, start the process and then measure your results, whilst addressing any issues that you had not considered previously.

On many occasions in a team setting I've identified changes that are needed, however other managers have not been keen on implementing changes and have opted to defer implementation until the next month, quarter, financial year etc. In these instances, whilst I did not have authority or control over what other managers decided for their teams, if I recognised the importance of the change enough then I would look to create plans, discuss the need and why with my team and implement the change earlier.

In all sales environments there will be periods where results are not where they should be. In one specific instance when this was the case, as a team we had anecdotally identified shifts in the market because of competitor activity and innovation, which was disrupting the traditional process. Knowing these factors was important, and even more so was the fact that the team had first-hand experience of their impact. Rather than continuing with the same ways of working and habits that everyone was used to, a change was needed now to improve results, as if we waited until the next month, quarter or financial year, there was no guarantee of success.

By changing our approach, re-evaluating the sales process and adjusting certain behaviours immediately, the team were able to react quickly, manage objections more effectively and collect more information on how the markets were responding to this change. Collating and analysing this information helped to further improve the sales process and behaviours that were needed to maintain our success in achieving our objectives.

Doing something 80% of the time maintains the habit

It's rare for anyone to complete the same activity in exactly the same way 100% of the time. Whenever a new habit is being formed it's important to continuously review and adjust the process until you're comfortable with it. When you start making the change, you're more likely to think about it more frequently which means you're focused, and soon enough the new habit has become your new norm. However, you might thereafter find yourself not always following the new way that you wanted to, and over time you may find that you're only doing it the new way around 80% of the time. It's fantastic that you've made this observation and recognised the deviation.

Whilst it's important to assess the 20% of time where you didn't follow the new habit, it's also important not to see it as a failure on your part. What has more than likely happened is that there have been new variables that you had not considered when you originally went through the planning process that need your attention. Forming a new habit takes time and doing it the way you want to 80% of the time is an achievement worth celebrating, and you're doing significantly better than if you had just ignored the change and maintained the old habit! I've often found that in this instance, to maintain or build momentum, keeping a journal to log your progress and assess the impact over time helps.

The impact of layering over time

Bad habits are formed through a lack of understanding, motivation or inability to see tangible results. More often than not, the bad habit will be tied to a trigger which activates an automatic urge to repeat an action or the habit. An example of this could be each time you pick up your mobile phone (the trigger) you check whether you have received any new messages or emails (the habit).

Unless we can understand and visualise the potential impact a habit is having on us, we're unlikely to want to change it, and even when we do realise its impact, we require a change in stimulus to motivate us towards wanting to make the change. This issue is compounded over time when one bad habit is formed and then another on top and so on. This layering of habits has an impact on an individual's ability to grow and develop effectively. This layering of bad habits is a significant contributing factor to why individuals fail to realise their potential.

Unsurprisingly, the opposite is true of when good habits are formed. When one good habit is layered on another, growth and development seem as though they are synchronised and there is harmony and fewer battles that an individual may need to overcome within themselves in order to realise their potential. This accelerates development and creates an appetite for continued growth.

Unravelling habitual programming

I recently worked with a call centre team that focuses on cold emailing and calling prospects to sell a range of products developed by the company. Their sales process mandates that every call or email sent should be logged into their client relationship management software. It has some inbuilt artificial intelligence technology that crunches information and helps build probability ratios for the sales director to use when forecasting and analysing results.

The process exists, as does the system, however the manager of the outbound calling team decided that it would be best for the team not to log their activity because it was impacting on their ability to make enough calls each day. The team were obviously overjoyed with not having to spend time updating the CRM system, and soon enough decided for themselves that there wasn't a need to log any email communication or even set up new customers through the CRM system. One bad habit had caused a ripple effect where the team layered multiple other bad habits with the justification of being able to generate more activity and better results. Each member of the team was using an Excel spreadsheet to keep a log of their prospects and bypassing the CRM system altogether.

When the sales director realised what was happening, I had been recruited to help implement a change programme and identify the best practice sales processes for the team to follow. The team wanted to achieve their team and individual targets; however, they had not realised the impact of their actions and behaviour on themselves, the team or the wider business. The manager who had allowed this way of working and the bad habits to form had left the company and the new team manager had been left to pick up the mess.

I identified other issues that this layering of habits had resulted in including:

- The stigma of recruiting individuals from this team because they did not follow the basic sales rules required
- Issues related to non-conformance of The General Data Protection Regulation
- Challenging to change the mindset and habits that had been formed, especially where individuals may now see a decline in commission earned

To unravel these habits and change the behaviour was a challenging and time-consuming process. When individuals are focused on themselves and do not understand the impact of their actions on the wider team or business, they lack the basic understanding and willingness to make the change.

Even when you can explain the issues and the reasons why changes need to be made, it's not a simple process to implement, as forming new habits will have an impact on the output as well as potential results that are achieved by the individual or group in the short term. In this case, when I explained to the team why the CRM system had to be updated and the importance of logging all activity, I found that the team became frustrated because they were now finding it difficult to achieve their activity targets as more time was spent on updating the CRM, which ultimately had an impact on their results.

Whilst the bad habits provided short-term success, they created a challenge for the business and a ripple effect within other teams. The time and energy it took to adjust the behaviours back impacted sales results adversely, which was avoidable had the right checks and balances been in place. In this and other similar situations there is no specific formula that can be applied to unravel the habits that have been formed. What I have found works best is to:

1. Identify the objective and what the desired outcome is.
2. Identify the root cause of the issues.
3. Understand the different points of view available.
4. Establish the impact of change to the individuals concerned.
5. Model out the scenarios, highlighting the potential impact of change.
6. Brainstorm with the individuals concerned the potential challenges and solutions.
7. Once their understanding of why the change is needed increases, map out the change process and start.
8. Monitor and measure impact of changes.

9. Re-evaluate the process for variations or the impact of new variables.

10. Continuously reassess and ensure process is fit for purpose to deliver the desired outcome.

Rather than seeing it as a one-off exercise, make it a continuous process and habit within itself. This will ensure processes remain valid and there is a constant self-checking mechanism in place.

Re-evaluate your decision-making criteria

In order to assess why the team had ended up where it was and had chosen to implement some of the changes, I decided to interview several members of the team to understand their perspectives. What I learned, as suspected, was that there was a lack of understanding within the team with regard to the impact and they had not thought through the implications of their decisions. The team manager himself had only been in the role for a short period of time and had made decisions in isolation without thinking about the bigger picture or discussing with his sales director.

Whilst the experience was challenging and tough for the new team manager and sales director to go through, it did provide both them and the rest of the business with an incredible lesson on the considerations that need to be thought through before any change in process is implemented. Decisions that are taken in isolation and without due consideration to the impact on other teams or the bigger picture often, in my mind, lead to challenges further down the line and create unnecessary work and hostility between teams and individuals.

Retraining and conditioning

The process of adjusting behaviours and retraining to form the right habits and behaviours took several months to unravel and for the team to understand what the impact of their actions had been. Getting them to see things from a perspective they had not considered, as well as highlighting the impact it could have potentially had on them personally if they were considering an internal promotion or looking at a job externally, helped to shift their attention and raise the importance of the change.

Once I was satisfied that they understood the habits they had formed were not right, we worked together on determining what the new processes should be and how they should be implemented. Each member of the team had the opportunity to input and was given the chance to ask clarification questions to ensure they understood why these changes were necessary. Eventually what they ended up with was a process similar to how the other teams in the wider business worked. This was documented and shared to ensure transparency.

I checked in with the sales manager and team leader several weeks later to see if the process was being maintained, and it was. I made a point of explaining to the team leader that every time a new person joins the team the same process needs to be applied to ensure their adoption and understanding of the process.

Working with this team who were willing to change made my work easy; however, it's not always the way. I've been in situations with more experienced salespeople where habits have been ingrained for years that needed to be changed, but the desire and motivation to do so wasn't there. In these situations, there are many more objections to handle and the time to adjust habits can be considerably longer as the individual needs to understand their own barriers to change. There is no guarantee they will change everything, but acknowledging the new process and way of working is a start towards that. The earlier that bad habits are identified and corrected, the better it is for the individual, the team and the business.

Chapter 6 Reflection Time

1. Are there any habits you can identify that you would like to change? What strategy will you adopt and how will you plan out the process to increase your chances of success?

2. When you're giving feedback don't use the word 'but' and instead replace it with 'and' – employees have been conditioned to only remember what the manager says after the word 'but' and none of the positive elements mentioned previously.

3. There is never a right time to change a habit, however procrastination only increases the chance of the issue snowballing. Once you've recognised a change is needed, conduct the necessary planning, due diligence and make the change.

4. If you're able to maintain a new habit 80% of the time, you're doing great. Just remember to go back and evaluate any new variables that you may not have originally considered.

5. Unravelling bad habits can take time. The key to success is identifying the root cause of the issues and then involving the individuals in designing what the new habit should be. The more they understand and the more invested they are, the greater the chance for success.

Chapter 7

IMPROVING FUTURE OUTCOMES AND DECISIONS

Experience and hindsight are wonderful things, especially when they leave an impression which you hadn't foreseen or expected. There is a lesson to be learned in every experience we have, regardless of whether we see it as positive or negative. Each adventure, so to speak, leaves us with a resounding message which, if we're prepared to listen, can help us and have a positive impact towards future decisions and their outcomes. No matter how similar a situation we think we are in, there are likely to be differences to the previous event that we are comparing it to, along with a range of different variables which are impacting on it. Our minds are great at creating associations and connections that make us feel comfortable or vulnerable when we feel like we are in a similar situation. Past experiences are an excellent way to help us plan better, ask questions to reduce the volume of assumptions, and develop models to identify what the outcomes could be.

In 2006, I made my first attempt to set up my own business and failed miserably. Whilst I had many years of working experience,

I lacked the execution skills and decisiveness needed, and rather than doing something that I was passionate about I was looking to copy a friend's (Bob) online retailing business. I was fortunate in that Bob was willing to share his knowledge and experience to help me, however that wasn't enough to ensure that I succeeded. I realised afterwards that I had no real plan and was trying to leverage Bob's experience and expertise to build my business on, which was unworkable and doomed to fail from the start.

This indifferent experience highlighted to me what I was lacking and needed to address before I could consider trying to set up my own business again. Twelve years on, with more experience, understanding and after developing a range of skills, I tried and have successfully set up my own business. This time, rather than copying someone, I've started a business that I'm passionate about and allows me to use my values and knowledge to help others. My consultancy practice, which aims to help businesses grow in a sustainable manner through better sales leadership and development of robust processes, gets me excited to wake up each morning knowing that I'm still learning whilst being able to help businesses and individuals realise their growth potential.

Each experience we have helps us, and whilst it's not always clear to see how at the time, when we take a step back and reflect, we're able to see the lesson we needed to learn in order to improve our future outcome and results.

Situational awareness

The term situational awareness relates in very simplistic terms to knowing what's going on around you. I went through a period of reading countless fictional books themed around the US Navy Seals, British SAS, Russian Spetsnaz, etc. In these books the concept of situational awareness was a running theme, whereby soldiers, to successfully complete their missions, had to always be on high alert and in a state of constant readiness. I became intrigued by the idea and started to relate to it from a business and sales context, and came to the realisation of how important the idea is when we're trying to understand many different perspectives, whilst constantly processing the impact of new variables.

Developing a situational awareness is a continuous process and something I trained myself to try and do. Working in a fast-paced commercial department where there was constant change meant that there was always a need to be alert and ready to react as something unexpected was always around the corner. If I wasn't alert to the potential changes, my mind would not be ready to react, and my reflex would have been slow at responding to the needs of those around me. This could have led to a knock-on impact on results the team and business were pushing to achieve.

Through identifying with this term, I started to become more aware of the different variables at play, with time being one of the most important ones. I realised how time poor and overburdened my team were with non-sales-related administrative requests from across the business, which whilst useful, was having an impact on their ability to focus on the key objective of either generating new sales or effectively managing existing accounts.

I observed and started to constantly monitor the performance of those around me and how they were reacting to unusual or new situations where they were asked to provide support. My heightened awareness, with regard to this and other similar situations, allowed me to connect the dots quicker and know when something wasn't right or where a proactive conversation was needed to mitigate against issues becoming chronic.

This wasn't about me trying to control everything, but a way of working that supported growth, development and gamifying the work environment to remove the monotony that can sometimes take over. It's easy to suffer from situational fatigue, where you're overthinking things. I knew I couldn't control everything, and I was comfortable with that, but what I was equally aware of was that I had developed a way of working where my reflex meant I reacted quickly, and my starting position tended to be two or three steps ahead of those around me.

Similarities and patterns

As I became more and more comfortable with the idea of situational awareness, I learned how to observe the similarities and patterns with how I reacted, my team reacted, as well as individuals within the wider business. Whilst situations may differ, the impact and release of positive or negative stressors tends to be transmitted in a similar way.

I remember two team members, James and Julia, having an issue with one another and an argument erupted on the office floor; they both felt the other was in the wrong, and in that heated exchange they were not willing to listen to each other's version of events. Rather than trying to resolve the issue there and then, I asked them to take some time out to calm down, write a brief summary of what happened as they saw it, and then we would have a conversation together later to discuss. I spoke to them separately to understand their respective views and thereafter we had a meeting together to discuss the issue.

Whilst most managers would have done the same thing, what my situational awareness and experience gave me was readiness to tackle the issue head on. I had been observing both individuals closely because they were new to the team, and had noticed their body language and an undercurrent of disdain in their conversations prior to the heated exchange. I knew that what had happened wasn't just about that particular issue; it was an excuse they had both used to release their frustrations. The underlying matter was something un-work-related altogether and the result of a misunderstanding on both James' and Julia's part. They were embarrassed with what had happened, however a good lesson for them with no long-term damage done.

Seeing patterns in behaviour and how individuals react helped me adjust my tone, approach and most importantly the questions that I asked. The more I practised and allowed myself to do this, the more I started to see things that I hadn't realised before. Whilst I observed so many behaviours, I rarely spoke about them with any of the individuals in question as I didn't want to pre-judge them. This was information that helped me improve the questions I asked and my understanding of the needs of those around me. The situational awareness meant fewer assumptions and more targeted conversations, which led to better results all round.

Asking the right questions

There is no such thing as a quick conclusion. If you simply apply historical experience to an issue today, you may generate a level of results. However, without using that experience to ask the right questions, you're unlikely to achieve the results that are possible.

In one of my first account management roles I remember being asked to prepare an account plan and was provided with a document detailing exactly how this should be done. I didn't understand the need for it, why it would be useful for me or how it would be used by the business. I asked these questions of my line manager, who unfortunately didn't explain the rationale and instead reiterated the fact that it needed to be completed and was a requirement for each salesperson. The fact my line manager didn't explain the why wasn't helpful to me because at the time I wasn't able to see the benefit of the task or how it could help me. I was left feeling confused and thought that this was an administrative task only. I completed the plan, however without the understanding and context didn't believe it was useful to anyone.

Several years later, in my first team leader role, and having figured out the importance of the account plan for myself, I was asked to get my team to complete a similar exercise. I wanted to make sure I didn't make the same mistake that my line manager several years previously had made in failing to explain the rationale. I got my team together and we sat down to discuss the objective and I asked them several questions to identify their level of understanding of the task and its importance. The team, like me and my original experience, didn't realise the benefits of the account plan or how it could help them. Rather than simply completing the task, we brainstormed the benefits and how the plan could be used as a tool for them to manage their respective books of business.

Through this discussion I learned that the traditional format didn't work for most of my team, and rather than getting them to complete an exercise that they would never refer to again, it was better to redesign the plan to fit with their daily working practice. I spoke to my line manager and explained the feedback that I had collected from the team and recommended a change to make the task more relevant to how the team were working today. My line manager provided some additional context for me and stated that if certain specific pieces of information were still available on the revised plans then there was no reason not to make the changes the team had identified. I took this back to the team and they duly completed the plans in the new format that they had created, ensuring that they could proactively use them as well as providing the business with the information needed.

Experiences should be used to enhance outcomes and not applied because that was how it may have historically been done. All processes and activities need a constant refresh to ensure they are still relevant, and more importantly to recognise whether the understanding of why they are important exists.

Reacting with new experiences

Anything that is new and we may not have experienced before can intrigue, excite, and at times even concern us. New experiences should be embraced because they allow you to use the knowledge and understanding from previous instances to continue learning whilst having to come to terms with new variables that you may not have considered or had to deal with previously.

Regardless of whether you determine an experience to be good, bad or indifferent, they often help you see things from a different perspective which will help your growth and development. Assessing what made the experience positive or negative can help in how you manage new experiences. Appreciating the experience as something you need to go through in order to get to the next stage of your development can also help adjust your mindset, especially if you're seeing the experience in a negative way.

Reflecting before making significant decisions

I've mentioned how important having a reflective practice is, and it's critical to take time and consider all the information, perspectives, personalities etc before making any significant decisions. The one thing you want to avoid is making that decision on impulse as you're unlikely to have thought things through well enough. If you are situationally aware then you condition yourself to constantly process and reflect, which makes taking most decisions a lot easier, quicker and with greater decisiveness.

The skill to reflect is hugely underrated and undervalued in business and by salespeople generally. Reflection provides context where you can visualise the outcome based on past similar events, and determine how plans may need to be adjusted and how it made you and those around you feel. It provides an opportunity to analyse introspectively, self-assess and determine necessary changes or the direction that is needed to maintain your values whilst knowing the potential pitfalls that may lie ahead in waiting.

Taking decisions can be an exhausting task, especially when you're not prepared or have not had the opportunity to review and consider the information available. Through situational awareness and reflection, you develop a state of mind where evaluation becomes second nature and it's a natural reflex. This shouldn't be mistaken for second guessing, as this is a skill where your mind processes the various pieces of information available and provides context to help identify the impact of various outcomes.

Making decisions for the right reasons

In any business, depending on your role you will be asked to wear multiple hats, and as such you need to be clear on the basis for why you've made a certain decision. For an outsider looking in, it's easy for them to make a judgment and suggest that the decision has been made for selfish personal reasons; however, they rarely have enough information to come to that conclusion, but they may do it anyway because it's the easy thing to say!

As a sales leader the basis and considerations for all decisions I made was simple in my mind and was focused on three elements: the individual, the team and the business. Whilst these may sound exceptionally broad, they provided me with context and a clarity that meant I had a consistent basis for each decision that I was taking.

My style of management has evolved and transitioned from process focused to people focused over time. I have learned that you can have the best processes in the world, but without the right engagement, attitude, motivation and understanding there is no guarantee that the process will be followed let alone maintained. On the flip side, if you don't have the right process but do have motivated individuals who are engaged and with the right attitude, they will more often than not find a way to work around the deficiencies in the process to achieve the desired results, whilst creating new processes that are fit for purpose.

Another example is with regard to celebrating success. Individuals can be successful on their own or as part of a team; however, if you want to maintain the team morale, work ethic and culture it's important to put the interests of the team before any one individual. Each month when my team achieved the monthly target, we would acknowledge the results and celebrate by having a drink, enjoying a meal, getting doughnuts etc. Each month some individuals had excelled whilst others may have struggled. Either way I always considered it as a team effort where we worked through the tough times together and equally enjoyed the good times together too.

There were numerous occasions where individual performances were celebrated, but the team came before everything else to me. We did things together and for one another. Whilst we came from different backgrounds and had varying interests as well as our own ways of working, everyone accepted each other for who they were, and we worked towards the same team objectives. Keeping this message consistent was a powerful statement for what the team stood for.

Planning out the consequences

If you struggle with the idea of reflecting regularly, then take a blank sheet of paper and consider mapping out the various options and identifying the potential consequences and reactions that you may receive before making a significant decision. No matter how you see something, there is a strong probability that others around you may not concur entirely with your view.

To help with your planning and decision-making process it's useful to think through the scenarios, the consequences, reactions and thereafter determine how you would respond in each instance. Rather than assuming what you think may happen, the planning will ensure you're ready to react appropriately and will give you confidence in your approach.

The first time I had to let a member of staff go from his position was daunting and scary to say the least. I knew the decision was for the best for all concerned, as expected results had not been achieved. I role-played the scenario with my manager and thereafter on my own several times before I was ready to deliver the news. My manager asked me some questions to help me prepare and I used those to reflect on and plan responses accordingly.

It's one of the worst sensations and feelings I've had because I was responsible for recruiting the individual, and I saw it as a failure on my part that they couldn't transition their previous experience into the way my team operated. I saw it as a failure in my assessment during the recruitment process.

That experience and impact of the potential consequences led me to change how I interviewed, the questions I asked and the understanding of the competencies that were important for each role. Having to tell someone that you have to let them go from their job is an unpleasant feeling and not something I was keen on experiencing regularly.

Knowing when to get involved

Understanding when you should get involved or take a step back and letting things play out comes with time and developing confidence in your own abilities.

When managing other managers, it's natural for you to want the best for each individual, but this cannot come at the expense of their development or by unnecessarily getting involved in every situation. There is a need to give them space and let them learn what they need to, whilst coming to you as and when they have questions or need support. I am not a fan of micro management and do not believe this method of management provides others with the freedom they require to express themselves or learn more about themselves or how to overcome challenges. Experience in management provides you with an innate understanding of knowing when to get involved and when to take a step back.

One time I remember stepping back letting a new team member, Priya, manage the sales process and negotiation, which she was convinced was going to close. I had heard some of the conversations and wasn't as convinced as Priya was because I didn't believe enough questions had been asked, timings were unconfirmed, and several other assumptions had been made. Priya made several follow-up calls and sent emails, however the client was not responding and she feared the worst and believed the sale had been lost.

I took this moment to speak to Priya to review the process and the steps that had been taken. I broke down what the client had said and how she had interpreted this versus what else it could have meant from the client's perspective. I highlighted some of the information that was missing and questions that could have been asked to support the process and improve her chances of success. In doing this, Priya's eyes were wide open and she realised there was so much more that could have been done.

There is no guarantee in sales, however the better your questioning and understanding of the client's needs, objectives and their desired outcomes, the more information you have to tailor your proposal and find the right hooks to support the sale.

Priya was a hunter. She took what she had learned and understood from our conversation and changed tactics with the customer to re-engage. Priya constructed a nicely worded email, highlighting some of the assumptions she may have wrongly made and asked for a call to clarify those points and discuss alternative solutions that may be more relevant. The client duly obliged and did respond, and although the sales cycle was longer than anticipated, the deal did eventually close.

It's OK to make mistakes

Mistakes are like miscalculations when we haven't got the right tools, information or experience and therefore act or make a judgment call that results in an adverse result or reaction to what was expected. Each time this happens, an opportunity is created to learn from and enhance our knowledge. Creating an environment where mistakes are used to learn from is invaluable for everyone's growth and development.

On many occasions I've witnessed first-hand sales managers who promote a culture of learning; however, when mistakes are made, they often at times belittle their team members rather than providing the necessary support and advice to help them learn and grow from the experience. This behaviour of promoting a culture which sounds like a good idea, but not acting in accordance with it, results in managers losing their credibility and respect. Furthermore, this type of behaviour tarnishes the environment that has been created and individuals tend to withhold information more because they do not want to find themselves being treated in the same way as their peers were.

On several occasions either I personally or my teams have come close to losing deals because I believe in the importance of having the right environment and doing things in the right way. There is value in managing an open transparent dialogue where you can use the environment that has been created and scenarios that present themselves to learn from. I've found that it breeds confidence in the team and fosters a culture where they are willing to experiment with new ideas that may not be natural to their normal way of working.

Using mistakes as an opportunity

Rather than sweeping bad news stories under the carpet, I was a supporter of using them as examples to inform, educate, improve and inspire my team. When something doesn't go as planned you have inadvertently got everyone's attention, which can be a challenge at the best of times. Using this opportunity to improve understanding and together discussing what happened and what could have been done differently has a huge impact. In these scenarios, team members are more than likely talking about the situation amongst themselves and Chinese whispers are likely to spread; so rather than letting them develop unrealistic conclusions, take the opportunity to share and change their mindset and thinking accordingly.

There was a team member, Max, who wasn't following the sales process and being transparent about certain aspects of the service the company was offering. Whilst there was no contractual need to inform customers about this particular nuance of the service, as a team we had decided to be open about it because we felt it was in the best interests of all concerned. One of my managers, Meghan, was contacted by some disgruntled customers who were not happy with the service and lack of transparency that had been provided. The manager and I spoke about the situation and agreed that it was best for her to speak to Max, discuss the complaint and what the impact was and would result in if he carried on in this way.

Meghan collected the information necessary, planned out her conversation and spoke to Max. At first Max was very defensive and not willing to admit and own up to his mistake. However, when the information on the complaint was referenced, he admitted to it and backed down. Meghan took this opportunity to explain to Max why not informing the customer was wrong and why they were compelled to complain about it. Max acknowledged his error and understood. However, Meghan didn't stop there; she went on to detail out the impact of this issue, not to the team, or the company, but on Max's reputation directly.

She painted the scenario whereby the customer who had complained left that company and joined another larger competitor in a bigger capacity. If Max had identified this larger competitor and was pitching to them and their paths crossed again, what did he think was likely to happen with the sale? The customer would have remembered their experience with Max, and based on this there was a chance that they would have opted not to buy because of that indifferent experience. Now if this situation was extrapolated to represent each customer who Max may not have been transparent with now, or in the future, what would the result be? The company would have lost the sale, but the impact on Max's personal reputation and confidence would have been far greater.

It's always about your team

When something goes wrong you must take responsibility, but at the same time when something goes right it's best to let the team or the relevant individuals within your team take the credit. As a manager or leader, it's your responsibility to enhance their credibility and boost their confidence in seeing what the impact and opportunity is if they can continue to deliver results and grow.

Managers need to be acknowledged, thanked and rewarded for their contribution, however the biggest measure of success will always be your team's performance. If the team delivers consistent results whilst navigating the challenges well and growing the business, then the manager has ultimately done their job.

Creating the narrative to support the direction of travel

Another important factor when using your experiences to improve future outcomes and decisions is your ability to create stories which the business or your team can relate to, understand and visualise. By helping individuals visualise the impact through stories you will have a better chance of them understanding how their behaviour needs to evolve and what your expectations are of them.

In my experience of managing teams, translating strategic vision and goals into operational and commercial objectives that are measurable and the team buy into is pivotal to success. Developing an ability to tell stories to support the team's understanding and helping them see what could happen helps to inspire them and focus their minds on the objectives at hand. Furthermore, being consistent about what the goal is and why it's important for the business, team and individual is equally important.

The goal is to get them excited, motivated and focused whilst delivering the commercial objectives required, and there is no better way of doing this than by painting an image of what the future could potentially look like.

Giving the context behind the decisions

By consistently explaining the context and rationale, the better the chance of individuals understanding the why and what the expectation is of them. Empowering individuals and trusting them with information helps them make better decisions, which will result in improved and more considered solutions being developed in the future.

In my experience, the more information I shared with my team, the better informed they obviously were, but more importantly they were able to appreciate the reasoning with why certain decisions had been made. They didn't need to agree with them but understood that based, on the choices available, why one was selected over another.

Addressing the cynics in the room

No matter how well thought through your idea, there will always be someone who is cynical about it or not completely convinced. More often than not this will be someone more experienced and may have been told a similar story or asked to do something like this in the past. Rather than letting your meeting with the group turn into a debate, identify those cynical individuals and discuss the idea with them in advance. Give them an opportunity to raise their concerns and tackle the objections at that point whilst asking for their support. Just because something similar may have been done in the past does not mean that it cannot be tried again. On the previous occasion it may have been the wrong timing or execution may have been poor – timing is crucial.

These cynics are experienced and have a point which is worth acknowledging and reviewing to ensure that your solution is executed correctly with the appropriate due care and attention required. On many occasions when I had what I thought was a great idea, I would speak to someone cynical because they were more than likely going to tell me something I may not have considered, and that would improve the robustness of the idea.

Showing versus telling

I had a simple rule: I wouldn't ask my team or anyone else for that matter to do something that I wasn't willing to do myself.

I've experienced situations where I've asked my team to do something and explained why, however they have been nervous or unsure as to how to go about it. If after some time they are negotiating with themselves and trying to compromise, rather than letting them get into a state of flux, walking with them on that road and supporting them on how it's done, whilst explaining the rationale and what happens if you don't do it or what happens if you cut corners.

There can be a disconnect that develops between team members and managers, where managers can lose credibility when they constantly keep demanding things. It's important to get your hands dirty and show individuals the how from time to time.

Additionally, each person's learning style is different, and whereas some individuals may be able to process written instructions, others prefer a more practical approach where they shadow and mimic actions to learn. There is no right or wrong way as long as the understanding comes with the relevant approach.

Chapter 7 Reflection Time

1. Observe and identify the similarities and patterns with how your team or colleagues react based on your approach. What changes can you make with how you react to elicit a different response?

2. Use your previous experiences to ask more direct questions, and then if required reflect before making any significant decisions.

3. Consider mapping out the different scenarios, potential consequences and reactions you may receive to help you plan better.

4. Use mistakes or situations where something has gone wrong as opportunities to learn from or to develop the team, processes etc.

Chapter 8

TAKING A DECISION IS BETTER THAN NOT MAKING ONE

I'm sure that there are thousands of examples of where not making a decision has actually been the best thing at a given moment in time. However, often it's not because someone consciously decided not to make a decision but instead something changed and in that moment of procrastination the decision was made for them.

In my opinion, procrastination for the fear of failure is a sin in business terms. If you've completed the appropriate due diligence and worked through the available information, reviewed the different perspectives and identified the risks and rewards, then the longer you procrastinate, the more likely that opportunity has a risk of failure. I appreciate that some will say that if you're unsure then you should step back and not take the decision. My argument is, and always will be, that if the work has been done and evidence suggests an opportunity or opportunities in certain directions, then timing is of the essence, and the longer you take to contemplate the various what if scenarios and possibilities, the more time you're giving to both existing and new variables changing the impact on the outcome.

I appreciate certain decisions require more time to reflect on because of their potential impact and the knock-on consequences, but let's be realistic, as a majority of those types of decisions are made by a committee in larger organisations, which slows them down! Within sales teams or smaller sales-led businesses, the opportunity to be nimble and progressive lies in the ability to make decisive decisions.

Imagine two businesses faced with the same decision about their respective products in a competitive marketplace. Both businesses have completed their assessment and there are advantages and disadvantages of making changes. The sales manager of business A can't decide what to do and as a result sticks with what he knows best and decides to make no change; whereas the sales manager of business B believes that something needs to be done and so she decides to experiment in the marketplace and allocate some budget, in doing so to test the reaction and impact. Without knowing the results, which business and sales manager do you think made the right decision? In my mind the sales manager of business B made the decisive choice and acted on the information and analysis that her team had collated.

Once you have information and decide to do nothing with it, you've accepted status quo and are too worried about impact as opposed to opportunity. Business B through testing and venturing in the market are likely to learn and validate whether the information they collated was relevant or not. Furthermore, they are likely to have understood more about the change that's taking place and have a different set of questions to now focus on. Regardless of whether the experiment that business B conducted had an impact or not, they would have a better foundation to move forward from, whereas business A will still be waiting to decide what to do next.

I appreciate that there are many factors that need to be considered, however if you believe in the individuals you work with, the teams that you have developed and the analysis that has been completed, then taking the decisive decision is a positive next step. I accept that in larger businesses more scrutiny is needed because the risks are far greater, but at the same time they have significantly more resources at their disposal to undertake further analysis, should it be required.

Learn by taking decisions

When someone fears making a decision it's typically because they don't want to get something wrong and the potential anxiousness that comes with failure. However, the best way to learn is to take decisions and if necessary adjust as needed thereafter. After you've done all the necessary work needed to put yourself in that position, it's important to take the next step and see it through. If you consistently do the analysis but then don't make a decision, you get into a cycle where you're questioning the value of the work you're doing as well as the purpose of the project in the first place.

From my own experience, taking decisions and then learning from the process was an incredibly powerful and introspective process which improved my confidence and helped me understand more about business and what broader considerations need to be made beyond what you know within the confines of your role. When someone trusts you to take a decision, you start to operate in a different way, where your level of responsibility has increased and you realise what the impact of not getting the decision right is. The weight of responsibility when taking decisions which impact more than just yourself can sometimes feel heavy on your shoulders; however, it's nothing to fear and more an acknowledgement of how far you've come on your journey and an opportunity to continue on that path of growth and development.

What taking decisions does

Making decisions and taking on that responsibility is empowering, and like with anything that will challenge you it will ultimately help you to grow. When you're required to make decisions, it enhances your capability to start seeing newer perspectives that you may not have previously considered, and there is greater clarity in wanting to know what impact the decision may have as well as what the desired outcome is. All these elements lead to further self-development and an adjustment in how you prioritise, the questions you will ask and even a review of the values that are important to you.

We all make decisions that impact on ourselves, but when you only have to answer to yourself the effect is limited, and if you make a decision which doesn't work out then no one else apart from yourself feels the consequence. When you make decisions that impact not only yourself but those around you, start taking more time to consider the impact, because if you get it wrong the likelihood is that you'll be disappointing more than just yourself, which brings with it a set of other challenges and issues. Taking time to consider the impact when others are involved is not procrastination. It is the process of conducting the necessary due diligence before taking the decision.

Ever since I had to take decisions on behalf of the team, my thinking and rationale changed. The amount of time I gave to considering each decision increased because I had to get it right, not only for myself but for the sake of the team. Each experience enhanced my appreciation of the process and what needed to be considered, why and most importantly how to go about it. Saying yes or no is easy but being able to stand up, debate and justify why you made the decision if something goes wrong and then changing course is so much more important and valuable.

The impact of procrastination

I once worked alongside a manager, Melanie, who liked to take her time in making decisions. There was an undercurrent of frustration brewing within her team because background work had been undertaken to get projects to a place where the next step required a decision from her before they could move forward. Rather than trusting the judgment of her peers and the recommendations of the project team or asking clarification questions, Melanie felt the need to re-evaluate everyone else's work and the assumptions on which the project decisions were being made. This process would naturally take time; however, more than that, the project team felt as though they had wasted their valuable time and effort because the same exercise that they had been asked to do based on their expertise was now being questioned.

Observing this situation was equally frustrating for me because it felt like everyone was in flux waiting for decisions to be made rather than focusing on the work that needed to be completed. Melanie may not have realised but her actions meant that people saw her as a control freak and a barrier to business and growth. The delays in making decisions caused her more work, frustrated the project team as well as other stakeholders, and limited the amount of progress that was made by the team. The procrastination only stopped when Melanie left her role and the business, as her managers were either not aware of the issues or were content with the approach that Melanie was taking.

If Melanie had remained in the business, a good strategy to tackle her inertia would have been to speak to her directly and understand her point of view as well as explaining the frustrations of the project team. This is not an easy conversation to have, however rather than making assumptions or letting frustrations boil over, taking control and trying to make a positive change is key. If after that conversation things did not change, then the issue can be escalated and discussed with other senior stakeholders to support the required change.

I've also seen similar examples where managers procrastinate because they are worried about how to communicate a change to their team. Whilst there is an impact that needs to be considered, sometimes when the decision being made is in the best interests of the business and you're aware of that, you don't need to sugar-coat it and instead work on managing the impact or looking at what potential opportunities might lie on the horizon because of the decision. There is never a good time for delivering bad news, however being there to discuss it with the team and providing as much context as necessary to help their understanding is always useful.

Taking calculated risks

Whilst taking decisions is important, the associated risks need to be considered too. Rarely does taking a decision guarantee success. In my experience you can't always control the results, however you can control the criteria used to make the decision, therefore it's important to be sure of what's in your control and highlight the risk elements that aren't.

As previously mentioned, reducing the volume of assumptions should be a key consideration. However, you'll never be able to process or appreciate all of them and thus at some point taking calculated risks becomes a necessary skill that needs to be adopted. Calculated risks are where there is no guarantee, however the analysis and evidence that you've collected points in a particular direction and suggests a better than average chance of success.

I recently completed an investment questionnaire and was ranked as a 7 out of 10 level in terms of my attitude towards risk (10 being the highest). I found this interesting because when I had completed a similar questionnaire several years earlier, I ranked as a level 9 risk taker. Reflecting on this, I thought is it my propensity to take risks reducing because I'm getting older and less willing to put what I have on the line, or is there another reason? The fact that I'm not married and have no children suggested to me that there was another reason. What I concluded was that my ability to use my experience in similar situations meant that I was carefully considering the options I had available to me much more. Whereas in the past I would have tended to make an impulse decision, I was now taking time to evaluate the options and deciding on what risks were worth taking versus those that were random hunches without any reasoning. This made sense to me more because over time the impact of risks or taking calculated decisions versus hazards materialising had decreased. Maybe I was finally growing up and better able to manage the pitfalls and expectations around me and of me!

Gut feel or hunch

There are times when you instinctively have a sense of what decision you should take without the need for considering other opinions and facts. I often act on instinct and believe it's an important attribute worth developing if you have the understanding and capacity for it. However, when taking decisions, and especially when they impact more than just yourself, no matter how instinctive you feel about something, it's important to have some checks and balances in place to validate before taking the decision.

On many occasions when recruiting individuals, especially where there were internal versus external candidates being considered, it was difficult to measure external candidates in the same way as internal candidates. Therefore, I often created a competency matrix of the key skills that I was looking for from the candidate in the role and measured everyone against those. Whilst I knew the internal candidates, I wanted to try and remain objective, and this process helped me score the individuals according to a set criteria. I had created the competency scoring matrix to use because too often I found myself relying on my gut feeling and instinct in judging the suitability based on candidates' interviews, which, whilst helping me make a decision, wasn't great at providing me with the context necessary for the feedback that I would be required to give. Creating this type of scoring system allowed me to validate my internal gut feel and acted like a sense-checking mechanism.

Forcing decisions without consensus

With the right cooperation most decisions can be made to have a successful outcome, but this can be hugely energy sapping and a distraction. Trying to convince the team or pushing them down a specific route to get their cooperation provides a short-term result, but it can cause challenges further down the line. I would urge caution pushing for cooperation as the success achieved may only be for the short term and could come at the price of burning your team out.

A better approach where having the right cooperation can lead to success is by making decisions to prioritise certain tasks versus others that are a nice to do. In an ideal scenario, businesses would like their teams to be focused on doing all the tasks that have been identified. However, the unfortunate reality is that most initiatives are time consuming to implement and require significant planning, resource and cooperation, hence you need to select what you focus on and then give them time to understand, implement and master before asking them to take on newer initiatives that will require similar planning and cooperation.

Within several family-owned businesses where I have consulted, decisions are typically made because family members think of an idea, are convinced it's the right thing to do, and without the facts or analysis, they ask managers to implement the change. The manager, regardless of whether they agree or not, feels obliged to execute the request and update the rest of the team on what needs to happen, whilst gently reminding them of where the original request has come from. What the family member or manager rarely thinks about is the impact on the day to day work the individual has been asked to do. There is an unwritten rule whereby the other daily duties remain a priority and will still be required to be completed along with the new request.

Whilst the family member may have a right in making such requests, the manager in that situation needs to be strong enough to ask the right questions and understand the objective, purpose and timelines whilst communicating the impact that this 'distraction' could have on the business and the team's workload. I've observed this urgent request or idea syndrome is always given a priority because of where it originates from, yet nobody asks the important questions to understand what the objective is or the potential desired outcome that is being sought.

Rather than making decisions and forcing cooperation, in my experience it's best to understand the objectives and then ask how the team could manage it and what the potential impact would be. I've found that this collaborative approach, where they are part of the decision-making process, helps them understand the need and ask the questions that they feel are appropriate or need clarification on. They are then more committed to ensuring the task is delivered along with a limited impact on their day to day work or by deprioritising non-urgent tasks.

Communication is key to effective management

It's no secret that effective communication is one of the most important building blocks for success. So why is it that so many individuals, teams and businesses struggle to implement and promote this vital skill?

I am an advocate of both transparency and open communication, however that is as a result of past observations and being in a team where communication wasn't forthcoming. Where communication is limited or there is a lack of information shared, individuals tend to make assumptions, connect their own dots and develop negative storylines and themes about both the team and business. If you then consider multiple individuals doing this and exchanging their theories, it's easy to see where a toxic environment can materialise from. When I first saw this type of behaviour, I wasn't experienced enough to understand it; however, at a later time when it made sense, it was obvious to me that where managers don't communicate and provide a platform for open dialogue, the void is filled with unanswered questions, assumptions and negative thoughts.

Involving teams and stakeholders

Making the right decision, for the appropriate reasons to benefit the team, business and that will support the attainment of the desired outcomes, can be challenging. I found that whilst the burden of responsibility might have rested on my shoulders to make the decision, how I went about that process of delivering the verdict had a significant impact on the team's commitment and the results we achieved.

In my experience, you need to take the team on a journey and show them the process you have gone through as well as what you hope the results will provide.

On one occasion a company I worked for was rebranding a product and with it launching new features whilst removing some redundant ones that were not adding value. Rather than just sending an email communicating the change, which may or may not have been read and understood well enough, the project team opted to get different departments that were impacted together and use it as an opportunity to share knowledge and experience of what the change meant, along with the benefits to each team and how it would improve their work and what they would mean for customers.

This approach of involving different teams and letting them present to one another created excitement, built momentum and generated a unified message for why the changes had been made and the benefits they would bring.

There were some individuals who were unhappy with the changes, but this was to be expected even though the information had been shared in advance. Sometimes you just have to acknowledge that change is difficult for some individuals to process and accept!

Impact of not having the right cooperation

Where there is a disconnect in communication and a lack of cooperation there often tends to be disharmony in and between teams with the scent of discontent filling the atmosphere. I've experienced a blame and cover your back culture developing where individuals protect their own interests rather than considering the broader impact on the team or business.

In one business where I consulted there was a disagreement between the sales team and the marketing team on how to execute an online ecommerce project. The marketing manager, Tony, wanted to implement a strategy of promotions and heavy discounting to generate interest, whilst the sales team unequivocally wanted to limit discounts offered to a minimum and reserve the option to provide one once an initial conversation had taken place with prospects that had requested a call back. The lack of cooperation between the teams created tension, where neither was willing to accept the other's proposal or even consider an alternative.

There were merits in both strategies but they were approaching them with two different sets of objectives and targets in mind, which was the root cause of the issue. Both teams ultimately wanted to support initiatives that would help the business grow, but because the basic communication and cooperation needed to understand one another's point of view was missing, the execution and implementation of the project was delayed for several months.

To think that a lack of communication is often the reason why a project is delayed, or objectives not being met, seems ridiculous, but it's a significant reason why growth stagnates within teams and businesses. Having a culture of open and effective communication ensures individuals, teams and departments are aligned, and encourages the questioning and challenging of ideas, which leads to better solutions and outcomes.

Chapter 8 Reflection Time

1. If you've completed the assessment and have put yourself in a position to take a decision, then see it through. Standing still and doing nothing will not change the outcome. Moving forward and experimenting or testing will validate the analysis and provide confidence in the next steps you take.

2. Use your instinct and trust yourself, however validate what you feel to ensure there is data to back up your course of action. Be consistent in your approach.

3. Avoid forcing decisions where you don't have consensus or stakeholders from multiple teams haven't been involved. Communication is key to effective management and execution of all initiatives.

Chapter 9

EVERYTHING YOU DO AFFECTS YOUR CHARACTER

The content from the topics discussed in the preceding chapters supports the advancement, stagnation or decline of your personal reputation and character. Everything you do or say, consciously or unconsciously, is either working towards building your profile and credibility or working against it. Perfection is a myth, and we should aim to be the best versions of ourselves whilst continually learning and improving from mistakes we may have made, working hard to maintain and uphold our values and setting the highest standards that we are willing to hold ourselves accountable to. Everything you do or say impacts on your character!

This is by no means an easy task and requires dedication, commitment and a willingness to look beyond the image that you see of yourself in the mirror or what others see. Given the society that we live in and the vast quantity of information that is readily available about each of us, it would be easy for anyone who wanted to obtain information (past or present), to put forward some negative spin and try to tarnish your reputation. You have limited control over this, and thus constantly focusing on doing your best because that is who you want to be, or see yourself as, shines through and allows anyone who is willing to listen or observe to see the real you.

When you strip everything away, all that is left is your credibility

Many of my one to one coaching sessions with team members would focus on this notion of developing your personal brand, reputation and credibility. I found that by relating it back to the individual and playing back their actions from the perspective of the client, their line manager or a senior member of staff helped them to appreciate how they were potentially being judged or seen by those around them. What they sometimes saw as trivial acts had much greater consequences for their personal brand reputation, as once a judgment had been made, that individual would always be measuring you against that benchmark.

My passion for this topic meant that when I was witnessing a team member doing something that could potentially impact on their character, I was keen to use it as an example to help them re-evaluate their own rationale and thought process towards not only the point at hand but more generally. My thinking is that if you remove the material junk we all accumulate and concentrate on who you are as a person, then you're able to see yourself differently and ultimately decide whether you like the person that you are. If you are comfortable with the person you see on the inside, then there is no need to fear that reflection resonating on the outside too.

Describe it as being true to yourself, or whatever works, but for me my thoughts, deeds and actions are a true representation of who I am, and what makes me the person I am. I have no need to try and fit in and instead am content with creating my own path to success and enjoying the lessons along the way.

You're always going to be judged

I would love to have developed this thought process from an early age, but my eureka moment didn't hit me until I was around the age of 30, more than 10 years ago. I was a worrier and would be concerned about people's perception of me and acted to ensure that I was accepted. This way of living meant that I became fearful of judgment and was doing not what I believed in but what I thought I should be doing to 'keep up with the Joneses'. Whilst it never manifested in me as taking decisions that went against my values, I kept questioning myself and wasn't happy with what I was doing.

I realised that regardless of whatever I do or say, I would be judged and had no control on whether anyone would see my actions and behaviour positively or negatively. I acknowledged for myself that I wasn't a bad person and was trying my best and doing things that I believed in and were of importance to me with consideration to those around me. My mentality changed and I stopped worrying about the fear of judgment because I couldn't control it. All I could control is what I did, how I did it and why I did it, and hence that became my focus. As opposed to wasting my time on what others may be thinking and doing, I started to work on myself and developing the person that I wanted to be and see in the mirror. I became more open to receiving feedback that allowed self-development, but was more cautious about who I asked for that feedback and instead identified individuals who, like me, were not 'followers' but trying to lead by example and change for the better.

Focus on doing things in the way that you're comfortable

We all learn, interpret and develop an understanding of information that is shared with us in our own way. Two individuals with differing levels of experience will interpret a request in a very different manner based on their understanding and level of comfort. With better understanding comes a level of experience in knowing how to respond in each situation, and in a manner where your values aren't impacted adversely.

As a new manager, I was once asked by my line manager at the time to advise my team that their Christmas leave would not be authorised unless all outstanding actions and customer orders were processed. Whilst I understood the message that my line manager was trying to convey, I wasn't comfortable with delivering it in the cold way that she had nonchalantly asked me to do it. At the same time, I didn't feel comfortable with broaching the subject with her because as I understood it, there was no room for negotiation on this.

Rather than delivering the message to my team, I asked each team member to prepare an update on what they had outstanding including next steps and associated risks. I went through the information with each person and we discussed the chances of processing the order or what fall-back plans needed to be in place. Rather than saying that they couldn't take leave if orders were not processed, I opted to use a more positive statement and instead said we can all have a good Christmas break and ensure that there is nothing distracting us at work over the holidays. We agreed a plan of action should the orders not be processed.

As it turned out, not every order was processed and several remained outstanding. I had provided my manager with the appropriate update and stated that although my team would be off during the period, they would attempt to contact clients and additionally I would remain available throughout to support them as needed. Although my manager was unhappy that not all orders had closed, she accepted the position and did not question the fact that I had authorised my team's leave regardless. I was pleased that I hadn't delivered her message as requested and instead used my discretion and what I was comfortable doing. Finding a compromise on delivering someone else's message but maintaining your own voice builds your confidence and upholds your values.

Manage what's in your control

A close friend, Ellie, recently started a new job working for a German food ingredients company, and just shy of her probationary period expiring, her line manager raised several concerns with her about her lack of visibility across teams, engagement within the team, exposure to senior managers etc. Ellie was pretty upset because, in her opinion, she hadn't been given the opportunity to put her best foot forward and show what she was capable of. Taking the feedback on the chin and rather than letting it overwhelm her, she decided to take control of the situation.

Ellie took each area of concern and developed a strategy on how to tackle the issue, identifying what she believed was needed to be done, as well as what assistance may be required. Throughout this process, Ellie maintained a fear that whatever she did may not be enough, but she persevered and tried to remain positive.

We spoke at length and my advice to her was to concentrate on the plan that she had devised, trusting her ability and focusing on the behaviour and actions that were natural to her and had provided success in previous roles. She had no control over what others said or did, but she did have control over how she reacted and responded to individuals regardless of the situation.

Five months later, Ellie had, in her manager's words, turned things around and was instrumental in helping the business secure a long-term contract with a client which was worth millions to the company. Ellie had originally started on a fixed term 12-month contract; however, eight months in and the company offered her a permanent position because of the value she had delivered. By focusing on what was in her control, Ellie let her results and success be the judgment as opposed to the feedback that her manager had suggested. Her attitude enhanced her reputation, which in turn led to the consequential successes that she benefitted from.

You can't coach attitude

I like a challenge and am willing to help most people. However, one challenge I haven't been able to overcome is where an individual has an attitude which detracts from the direction that you're taking the team in. A bad attitude creates a divisive environment and makes other individuals within the team uncomfortable. It's not easy to manage and can have a negative impact on the intended desired outcomes.

You can help an individual change certain behaviour through addressing their thought process on how they see situations and react, but I don't believe you can coach someone to improve their attitude or determine what is and isn't good moral conduct. This has to come from within the individual.

During the recruitment process, the questions that you ask or role-playing examples with an individual can provide some insight. Understanding how a person has reacted in difficult situations or how they would react in hypothetical scenarios and then cross-referencing the responses with the information on their CV or what they have shared in an interview can be a good indicator; however, it may not always be conclusive. Another strategy that I adopted from time to time was to ask the potential recruit to meet specific members of the team in an informal setting prior to making a final decision. Having an alternative perspective and seeing how they engaged in an informal environment sometimes helped confirm the decision.

Attitude and character are foundations for success and something that I look for in each person that I am working for or with. A person displaying a positive attitude and characteristics is more likely to succeed as well as supporting those around them.

Enhancing your attitude

Your mindset, values, reaction in situations, curiosity etc all play an important role in developing and enhancing your attitude and key characteristics. These are complex subjects, in their own right, that require a commitment to growth without the creation of boundaries or setting of time expectations on when they will be achieved.

The biggest investment should be in developing yourself, and with that will come a change in attitude as you appreciate yourself and those around you more. I worked with an incredibly talented lady, Becky, who had an infectious personality and attitude for learning and improving whatever she got involved in. The energy around Becky was special and drew people towards her to the point that when Becky was managing a project those around her wanted to be involved because they believed that if she was involved the chances of success increased exponentially.

When I spoke to Becky about this, she gave me a blank look. She was just being natural to herself and doing the things that she was comfortable with in her own way. Like many individuals aspiring to realise their dreams, Becky had made a conscious choice to continuously work on herself and knew that her attitude was what she was in total control of and could nurture to help support her aspirations and development. What others saw as amazing was Becky just being herself and trying to improve on every day.

There are some simple yet effective practices that everybody can adopt to enhance themselves. Respecting everyone's time and especially your team members', no matter how junior they are, is a great example. Not being late for meetings, rescheduling last minute or rushing around headless are others. These examples set the tone for the way that you expect them to respect you, and it shows that you truly value their time and what they're doing for you, so they are more likely to keep on doing it well. Being seen as stable, organised and approachable, instead of rushed and terrifyingly busy, brings with it a calmness which sets the tone and enhances your character.

Issue with attitude

I'm sure that we can all picture someone that we've come across who we believe has had a bad attitude. Those individuals are challenging to communicate with and we struggle to find anything in common with them. They tend to be a drain on your energy and every conversation seems like a battle.

I once found myself in a situation where I had inherited a team where I was overwhelmed with the negativity, adoption of bad practices and general disregard for those within and around the business. There were a couple of individuals in this team who were taking far too much for granted, including their experience and believing that because of their status they were untouchable, and the business would not have been able to survive without them. Their behaviour was having a damaging impact on the rest of the team and I knew that I couldn't let those practices continue.

These individuals I found were outwardly very confident and often showed aggression as a means of pushing their ideas or suggesting an aggregated impact if their ideas were not adhered to. They were argumentative to the point of being contradictory and twisted stories in whatever way necessary to ensure the outcome supported their selfish means. Another interesting observation I made was that when they tended to be doing something they shouldn't, they would go radio silent, trying to go unnoticed, however silence is sometimes the biggest indicator that something is wrong!

I reviewed each person's performance versus activity targets. The two individuals who had been challenging every decision and request unsurprisingly had the lowest activity rates within the team. They made no secret of their unhappiness at my insistence of measuring performance to understand where challenges were.

They were happy to continue to play the blame game and deviate attention away from themselves.

After a few months I started to see some patterns and anomalies emerging in the results for these two individuals. The metrics didn't make sense and so I investigated further and what I found was both interesting and concerning. On days where they had suggested that they were seeing clients, blank entries appeared within the CRM system against different customer records. Not wanting to make any assumptions, I took this to my boss to get his take on it and it was something that he had experienced before.

The individuals were creating erroneous meeting events and subsequent contact reports without meetings ever taking place. These individuals were given the opportunity to come clean, but even at that moment their arrogance and attitude stopped them from doing so. When the evidence was presented to them, you'd have thought that they would have been embarrassed and distraught, but instead they smirked, admitting nothing and happy to leave the business probably surprised at how long they had been able to get away with it.

This type of attitude cannot be coached, and whilst you can try to help individuals or even implement control protocols, when individuals have no regard for rules or those around them it becomes exceptionally difficult to manage them. It is because of the challenges that this type of situation brings that managers must be equipped to deal with conflict. I've seen many individuals shy away from similar situations because they don't know how to manage the conversations, and the longer it's allowed to carry on, the tougher it becomes to address. It's important to keep front of mind that you're making changes that are in the best interest of the team. Not addressing the issue creates doubt within the manager and sets the wrong example for the rest of the team.

To mitigate against similar situations spiralling out of control, as soon as there is a doubt or inkling of something not being right, I would recommend asking questions to understand the situation better and identifying where the issue stems from. The earlier you're able to address it, the less impact it will have. Most managers will know when something doesn't feel right and in that moment it's important to act on your instinct and ask questions to validate what you believe may be wrong. Leaving situations to chance is not an option and will lead to bigger and tougher issues down the line.

Seeking validation from those around you

When you're constantly working on yourself, it can be hard for you to evaluate whether you're going in the right direction and the impact your self-development programme is having. It can be challenging for you to analyse the impact of the changes you've made because we're likely to be more self-critical and not always notice the small subtleties that others who don't see us every day may be able to spot.

I've found that sometimes the best people to ask for feedback about the changes you've made are those in senior positions within your department or departments that your team works closely with. I find that because they are removed from the day to day engagement with yourself, they see changes with you quicker as well as their impact.

Furthermore, these opportunities to meet senior individuals within any department are fantastic because you're able to learn more about their thought process and experience. The perspective that they provide and their journey can help you build confidence in what you're doing. Every experience – good, bad or indifferent – if approached in an open and positive manner will support the development of your character and ongoing growth.

What others say about you enhances your credibility

Whilst self-promotion and personal branding is important, your character and credibility are enhanced tenfold when others within your team, department, business or even customers deliver positive affirmations, comments and statements about your working practices, attitude and behaviour.

When you write your curriculum vitae, it attempts to show the best of you in order to support your objective of gaining a promotion or moving into a new role. What has previously piqued my interest is when individuals have included endorsements from current or past managers within their CV. These statements are more powerful, and the words used to describe an individual tell a lot about where they are versus the self-promoting words used elsewhere in the CV.

Anyone who you engage and interact with who has a positive experience with you and shares that with others will enhance your reputation. If you're doing things for the right reason and not for the endorsements, which will come if you do the right thing anyway, then you'll probably find that your growth accelerates too.

I've asked past bosses about the process that they have undertaken when recruiting internal candidates and an important choice factor is what other team members and individuals have said. Whilst this is not the most important factor when making the decision, it's a good gauge to get a sense of what experiences individuals have had and whether the reaction has been positive or negative. If someone works in a particular way all the time, rather than just at a point in time because there is something on offer for them to work towards, that behaviour shows through when speaking to wider teams.

I mentioned my friend Ellie, who successfully turned around her manager's perception. At the point when she was offered a permanent contract, I helped her with trying to negotiate a salary increase. Ellie has always been uncomfortable in these situations and typically would negotiate with herself and ask for a lower amount than she actually wanted because she didn't think she'd realistically get the increase she wanted.

Rather than worrying about whether she thought it was realistic or not, I asked her to imagine that she was writing an email to her department director asking for the increase and justifying it. I asked Ellie to include the amount of the increase she wanted, include a list of reasons why she felt she deserved the increase including examples of the value that she had added, and where she had consistently gone above and beyond what the scope of her role was. Finally, I asked Ellie to collect some statements from her customers, both internal and external, about their experience of working with her.

Ellie prepared the email and sent me a draft to review, which we discussed, and she tweaked the structure slightly to make it a little more direct and enhance some of the stories of the impact that she had made. After doing this I asked her whether she still had any doubts about the figure that she was looking for as an increase. Ellie was positively shocked because the structure and format that I had asked her to follow, including the endorsements from clients, meant she now understood the value that she delivered and what customers and peers across the business thought about her. Those endorsements were like gold dust for building her reputation, and more importantly her self-confidence. Finally, I suggested to Ellie to set up a meeting with the department director and talk through the request using the email as a structural guide for the conversation and thereafter to send the email as a follow-up.

By going through this process, Ellie had collected the relevant information, developed a written response which formed the structure of her formal conversation, and thereafter she was able to use that email to follow up the meeting. When I caught up with her after the meeting, she was positively beaming because the director had acknowledged the value she had brought to the role and company, and whilst he couldn't commit on the spot, agreed that a salary increase was appropriate.

A couple of weeks later, Ellie received confirmation that she would receive the increase she had requested. At that moment she felt as if she should have asked for more; however, one step at a time, and it's important to be comfortable with the process and with what you're looking to achieve for yourself.

The power of endorsements

When your peers, a manager on another team or someone more senior acknowledge and recognise your contribution and hard work, it's very valuable and what they are saying is that they see you as an important role model who is contributing to the success of the team and helping to develop those around them.

This is a huge compliment and should provide encouragement to carry on what you're doing. I don't believe you can force people to do this; it has to come from within and the individual has to want to do it themselves. On many occasions I've spoken about the impact of this to individuals, and even though they grasp the concept, they fail to put it into action. Maybe it's because the results cannot be seen immediately or the dedication and change in behaviour that is needed is difficult to commit to. The most successful individuals do this as a habit and form a natural reflex to elicit this behaviour – not for any praise or kudos but because they believe it's the right thing for them and the best way to conduct business. The positive impact on your character multiplies significantly.

As individuals don't always know how to give feedback, you need to help them do this. A colleague designed a reflective exercise where at an annual team kick-off she passed a series of cards around to each person on the team. There was a separate card for each team member and the requirement was to list three things that they admired in that person. This simple yet effective exercise provided each person with an opportunity to reflect and recognise the positive contribution that every team member had made; at the same time they received a set of cards detailing the appreciation that colleagues had for them. I still have these cards in my drawer and they are a powerful reminder of the impact you can have in helping each and every individual around you.

A platform for continued growth

Do the best that you can until you know better, and then do better. Once you receive the testimonials and endorsements from clients or colleagues, it's a great time if you are ever suffering from a crisis of confidence to use these statements to focus, energise and push yourself forward. It's natural to sometimes be unsure about the reaction of others, however knowing the positive impact you've made can be used as a platform to work towards a higher standard for yourself.

I haven't come across anyone that doesn't like to be told that they're doing a good job. Everyone needs that affirmation now and again. Just as you can use it for your own growth, a simple well done, thank you or other positive statement can go a long way in helping your team remain motivated and committed to their own self-development. This appreciation of those around you supports your development too and helps connect you with your team on a deeper and more emotive level.

Dealing with negative feedback

For all the positive statements, from time to time there will be someone who receives negative feedback which they are unhappy with or disagree with. This needs to be assessed on its merit to decide whether it's fair and accurate. Whilst you never want to demotivate a member of the team, sometimes tough love is needed and using any third-party feedback to do this can add weight to your argument.

One time an individual on my team received some indifferent feedback from other teams in the business about the quality of his work. This coincided with him applying for a managerial position, however the two things were different and, I felt, needed to be managed as such. I'd gone through the competency assessment and scoring, and both his line manager and I felt another candidate was better placed for the role, and unfortunately this individual wasn't successful.

A few days later, his line manager and I went through the negative feedback he had received from the other team. He had been aware of this feedback at the time of the interview, and we had advised him that they were two separate issues and would be managed as such. However, now that he knew he hadn't been successful in the promotion, he was adamant that we had used the negative feedback to make our decision. I knew this was 100% not the case and used the competency assessment scoring to provide some honest and open feedback.

My point is that a person chooses to see something positively or negatively and they decide the reaction and next course of action. In this case, and having to listen to the reasons why it was our fault and not his that he hadn't been successful in the application, confirmed for me why we had made the right choice. The interesting thing about building character is that you can work hard, and you can change what you do and how you do it to alter people's opinions. Those that choose to invest their energy in making positive changes will thrive, whilst others keep blaming someone else for their lack of commitment to themselves!

We all have the capacity to build a distinctive character that makes us stand out from the crowd. I believe in constantly aspiring towards a higher or deeper mental and moral code of conduct that underpins everything that I do. There is no finish line in sight in this journey, instead continuous improvement and a commitment to myself and those around me to always try to do the best that I can and pushing the boundaries to develop a greater understanding.

Chapter 9 Reflection Time

1. Everything that you do impacts on your reputation and character, so ensure whatever you say or do, consciously or subconsciously, is working towards building your credibility.

2. You will always be judged, however that should not be your focus. Instead concentrate on what you're able to control and influence and do that to the best of your ability.

3. You cannot coach attitude; however, you can ask situational questions and then cross-reference those with other responses to test for consistency.

4. The biggest endorsement you can receive is from your team, peers and senior stakeholders. What they say about you enhances the character that you've developed.

Conclusion

Writing this book has been an exciting, challenging and thoroughly rewarding process. My hope is that it has persuaded you to start thinking more deeply about the topics covered and the potential benefits execution of the ideas could have for your continued success.

We all learn, grow and develop at a different pace and must interpret the topics and themes based on our level of experience, understanding of ourselves and where we believe we are in relation to where we would like to be and what we ultimately want to achieve. There is no limit to what we can accomplish, and the only barriers are the ones that we create for ourselves.

You may have managed to realise that this is not a book entirely focused on sales but about building character which will lead to excellence in sales leadership. If you're able to internalise these topics, then you'll be head and shoulders above anyone else.

If you're committed to your vision of growth and development then it's vital to acknowledge where you are today, identify what you need to move forward and thereafter plan the course of action that will enable you to activate your potential. Most importantly, do not leave your development to chance or in anyone else's hand. If the endeavour is important enough to you then take control and ensure that you're focused on:

- Appreciating your values and what you stand for because these have a conscious and subconscious effect on your outlook and the decisions that you make

- Always considering as many perspectives as possible whilst reducing the number of assumptions you make

- Identifying habits that no longer serve you and working to implement changes that will support your continued development and growth

- Using your experience to help you as opposed to hindering your progress; everything that you've been through is working to support your next move and stage of development

These topics balanced with traditional management and leadership skills are critical for success. I challenge you to analyse yourself and create new standards that you're willing to fight for and that you believe in because they are in line with the vision that you have created.

Just like some boxers use lemon juice each morning to cut through the first layer of fat before starting their workout, I hope that SLICE can pierce through the behavioural barriers and provide deeper meaning and focus to what it takes to breed success.

Ultimately, everything that we do or say, consciously or unconsciously, affects our character. Whilst we all make mistakes, it's what we achieve, maintain and manifest over an extensive period that creates the associations between how everyone perceives us versus the best version of ourselves that we want to be.

I encourage you to assess yourself introspectively, challenge the status quo and work towards executing the powerful vision that you're dreaming about for yourself.

About the author

Vinit's career in sales began over 20 years ago. He has amassed a wealth of knowledge and experience in a wide variety of commercial roles while working his way up the corporate ladder.

His expertise is in problem solving, analysing trends and scoping out new business opportunities as well as managing teams of different shapes and sizes. More recently, he was the commercial director for a large UK-based SME, where he developed his sales leadership skills and successfully implemented numerous change programmes.

He has a passion for building high-performance teams by inspiring, motivating and coaching colleagues and team members to deliver great customer experience whilst focusing on continuous improvement.

Vinit has an abundance of commercial and operational experience. This has helped him build a track record of creating sustainable value and delivering ROI by translating strategic objectives into innovative, commercially viable solutions. He excels at implementing complex change projects to enable step change or transformations with a long-term vision in mind, whilst setting direction at pace which provides clarity and focus with a fun, high-energy leadership style.

Vinit values and follows the principles of Jainism and is focused on improving his understanding and our impact on the world. He firmly believes in the importance of down time away from work and enjoys meditation to refocus his mind and relax. Vinit enjoys and partakes in a wide variety of sports, trying new food experiences and cuisines, travelling and learning about different cultures. He is an avid reader of both thought leadership and fictional novels and always looking for ways to improve himself and learn. He enjoys spending time with family and friends and each year plans experiences that will force him out of his comfort zone.

Printed in Great Britain
by Amazon